Collecti

This travel book is used on 5 week vacation. It includes 35 pages to record and store each day.
You can organize two trips. The first 3 weeks and the second 2 weeks for example.
You will only be gone two weeks per year on holiday but you go on weekend very often with family or friends? This book is for you!

Organize your trip

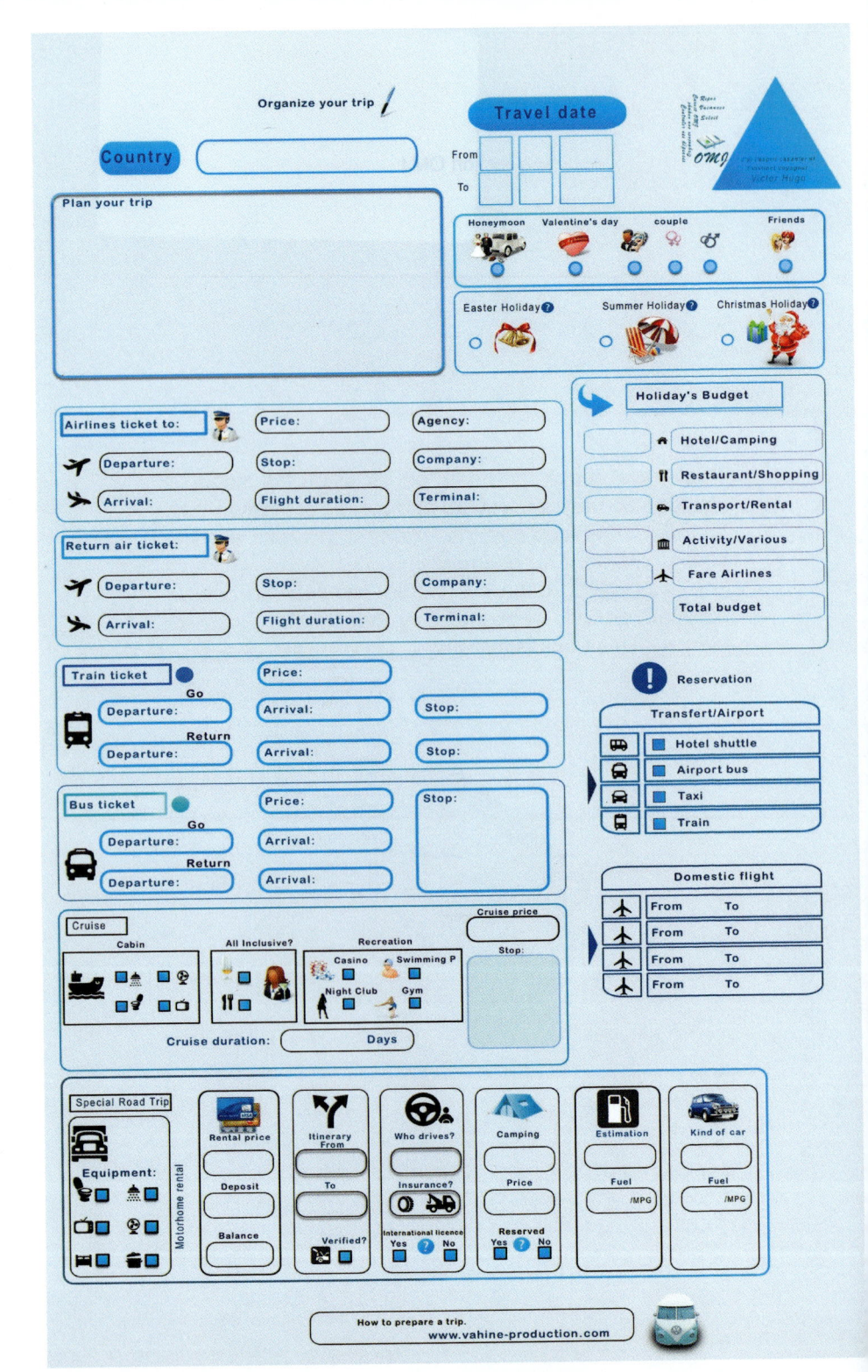

Country:

Plan your trip

Travel date
From
To

- Honeymoon
- Valentine's day
- couple
- Friends

- Easter Holiday?
- Summer Holiday?
- Christmas Holiday?

Airlines ticket to:
- Price:
- Agency:
- Departure:
- Stop:
- Company:
- Arrival:
- Flight duration:
- Terminal:

Return air ticket:
- Departure:
- Stop:
- Company:
- Arrival:
- Flight duration:
- Terminal:

Holiday's Budget
- Hotel/Camping
- Restaurant/Shopping
- Transport/Rental
- Activity/Various
- Fare Airlines
- Total budget

Train ticket
- Price:
- **Go** — Departure: / Arrival: / Stop:
- **Return** — Departure: / Arrival: / Stop:

Bus ticket
- Price:
- Stop:
- **Go** — Departure: / Arrival:
- **Return** — Departure: / Arrival:

Reservation

Transfert/Airport
- Hotel shuttle
- Airport bus
- Taxi
- Train

Domestic flight
- From To
- From To
- From To
- From To

Cruise
- Cabin
- All Inclusive?
- Recreation: Casino, Swimming P, Night Club, Gym
- Cruise price
- Stop:
- Cruise duration: ___ Days

Special Road Trip
Equipment:

Motorhome rental
- Rental price
- Deposit
- Balance

- Itinerary From / To
- Verified?

- Who drives?
- Insurance?
- International licence: Yes / No

- Camping
- Price
- Reserved: Yes / No

- Estimation
- Fuel /MPG

- Kind of car
- Fuel /MPG

How to prepare a trip.
www.vahine-production.com

Travel preparation

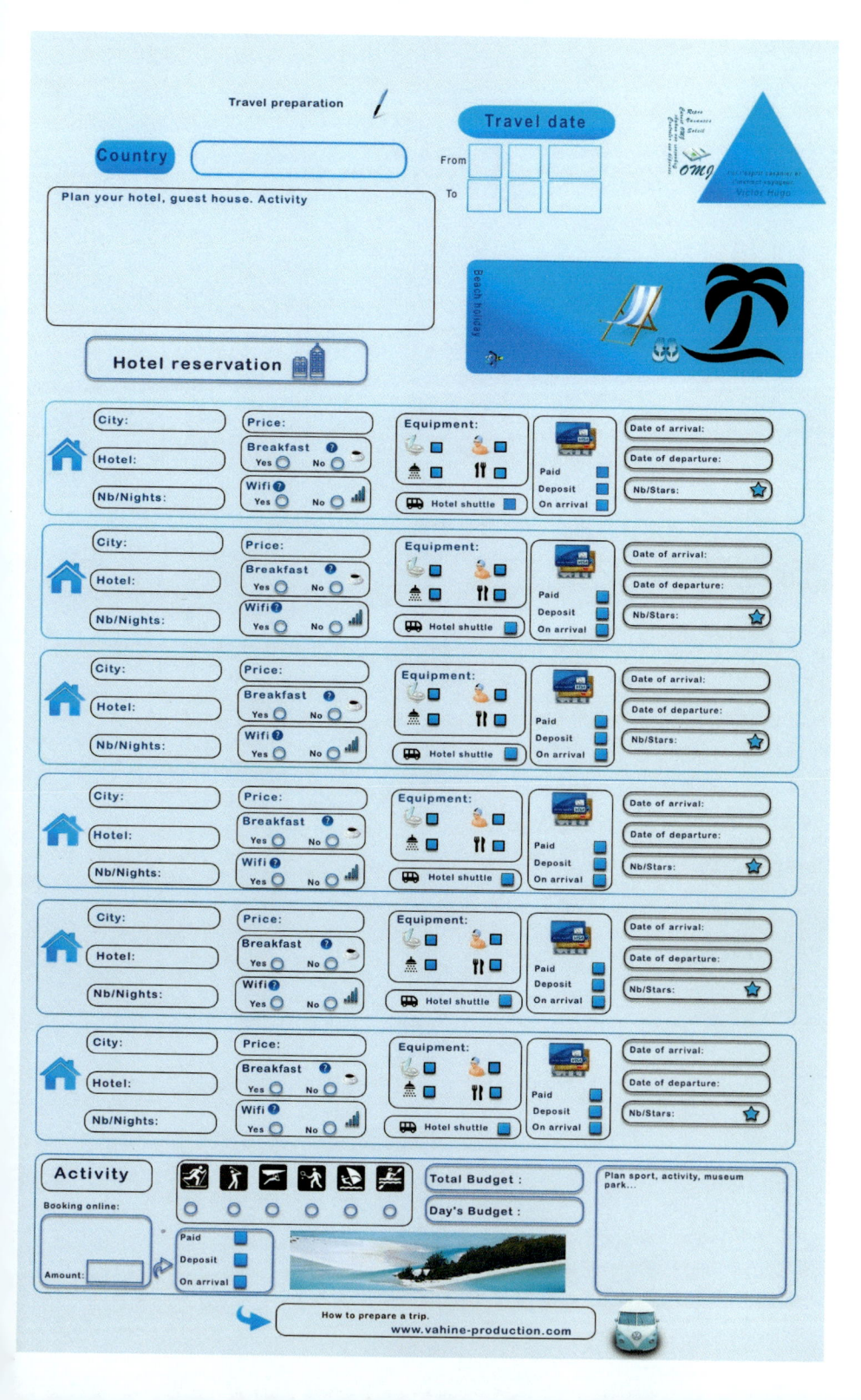

Country: _____

Travel date
From: ☐ ☐ ☐
To: ☐ ☐ ☐

Plan your hotel, guest house. Activity

Beach holiday

Hotel reservation

Entry 1
- City:
- Hotel:
- Nb/Nights:
- Price:
- Breakfast: Yes ○ No ○
- Wifi: Yes ○ No ○
- Equipment: ☐ ☐ ☐ ☐
- Paid ☐ Deposit ☐ On arrival ☐
- Hotel shuttle ☐
- Date of arrival:
- Date of departure:
- Nb/Stars:

Entry 2
- City:
- Hotel:
- Nb/Nights:
- Price:
- Breakfast: Yes ○ No ○
- Wifi: Yes ○ No ○
- Equipment: ☐ ☐ ☐ ☐
- Paid ☐ Deposit ☐ On arrival ☐
- Hotel shuttle ☐
- Date of arrival:
- Date of departure:
- Nb/Stars:

Entry 3
- City:
- Hotel:
- Nb/Nights:
- Price:
- Breakfast: Yes ○ No ○
- Wifi: Yes ○ No ○
- Equipment: ☐ ☐ ☐ ☐
- Paid ☐ Deposit ☐ On arrival ☐
- Hotel shuttle ☐
- Date of arrival:
- Date of departure:
- Nb/Stars:

Entry 4
- City:
- Hotel:
- Nb/Nights:
- Price:
- Breakfast: Yes ○ No ○
- Wifi: Yes ○ No ○
- Equipment: ☐ ☐ ☐ ☐
- Paid ☐ Deposit ☐ On arrival ☐
- Hotel shuttle ☐
- Date of arrival:
- Date of departure:
- Nb/Stars:

Entry 5
- City:
- Hotel:
- Nb/Nights:
- Price:
- Breakfast: Yes ○ No ○
- Wifi: Yes ○ No ○
- Equipment: ☐ ☐ ☐ ☐
- Paid ☐ Deposit ☐ On arrival ☐
- Hotel shuttle ☐
- Date of arrival:
- Date of departure:
- Nb/Stars:

Entry 6
- City:
- Hotel:
- Nb/Nights:
- Price:
- Breakfast: Yes ○ No ○
- Wifi: Yes ○ No ○
- Equipment: ☐ ☐ ☐ ☐
- Paid ☐ Deposit ☐ On arrival ☐
- Hotel shuttle ☐
- Date of arrival:
- Date of departure:
- Nb/Stars:

Activity

Booking online:
- Paid ☐
- Deposit ☐
- On arrival ☐

Amount: _____

Total Budget:

Day's Budget:

Plan sport, activity, museum park...

How to prepare a trip.
www.vahine-production.com

NOTE

NOTE

Organize your trip

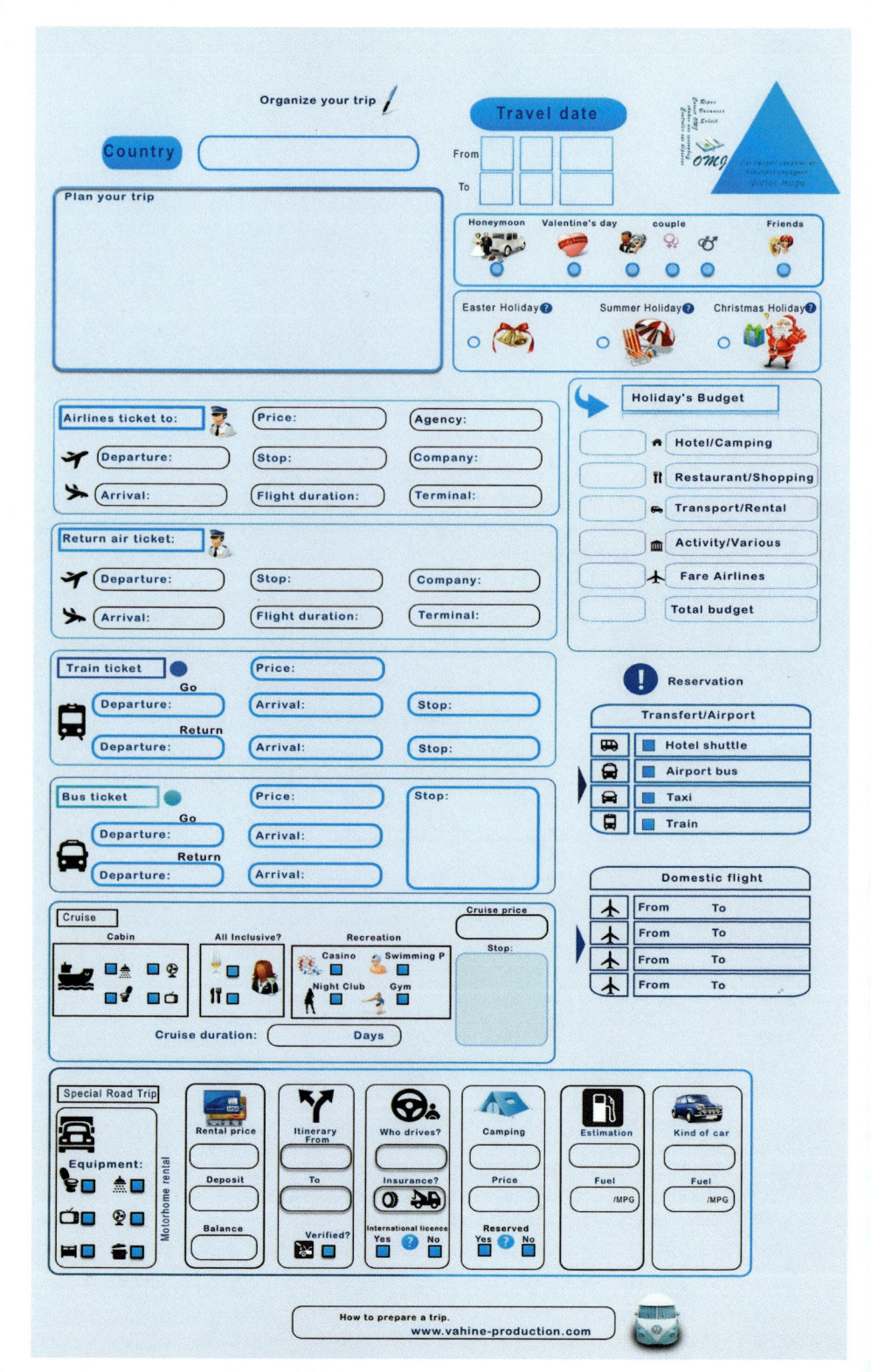

Country:

Plan your trip

Travel date
From
To

- Honeymoon
- Valentine's day
- couple
- Friends

- Easter Holiday?
- Summer Holiday?
- Christmas Holiday?

Airlines ticket to:
- Price:
- Agency:
- Departure:
- Stop:
- Company:
- Arrival:
- Flight duration:
- Terminal:

Return air ticket:
- Departure:
- Stop:
- Company:
- Arrival:
- Flight duration:
- Terminal:

Train ticket
Go
- Departure:
- Arrival:
- Stop:
- Price:
Return
- Departure:
- Arrival:
- Stop:

Bus ticket
- Price:
- Stop:
Go
- Departure:
- Arrival:
Return
- Departure:
- Arrival:

Holiday's Budget
- Hotel/Camping
- Restaurant/Shopping
- Transport/Rental
- Activity/Various
- Fare Airlines
- Total budget

Reservation

Transfert/Airport
- Hotel shuttle
- Airport bus
- Taxi
- Train

Domestic flight
- From To
- From To
- From To
- From To

Cruise
- Cabin
- All Inclusive?
- Recreation: Casino, Swimming P, Night Club, Gym
- Cruise price
- Stop:
- Cruise duration: _____ Days

Special Road Trip
Equipment:

Motorhome rental:
- Rental price
- Deposit
- Balance

- Itinerary From / To
- Who drives?
- Insurance?
- International licence: Yes / ? / No
- Verified?
- Camping / Price
- Estimation / Fuel /MPG
- Kind of car / Fuel /MPG
- Reserved: Yes / ? / No

How to prepare a trip.
www.vahine-production.com

Travel preparation

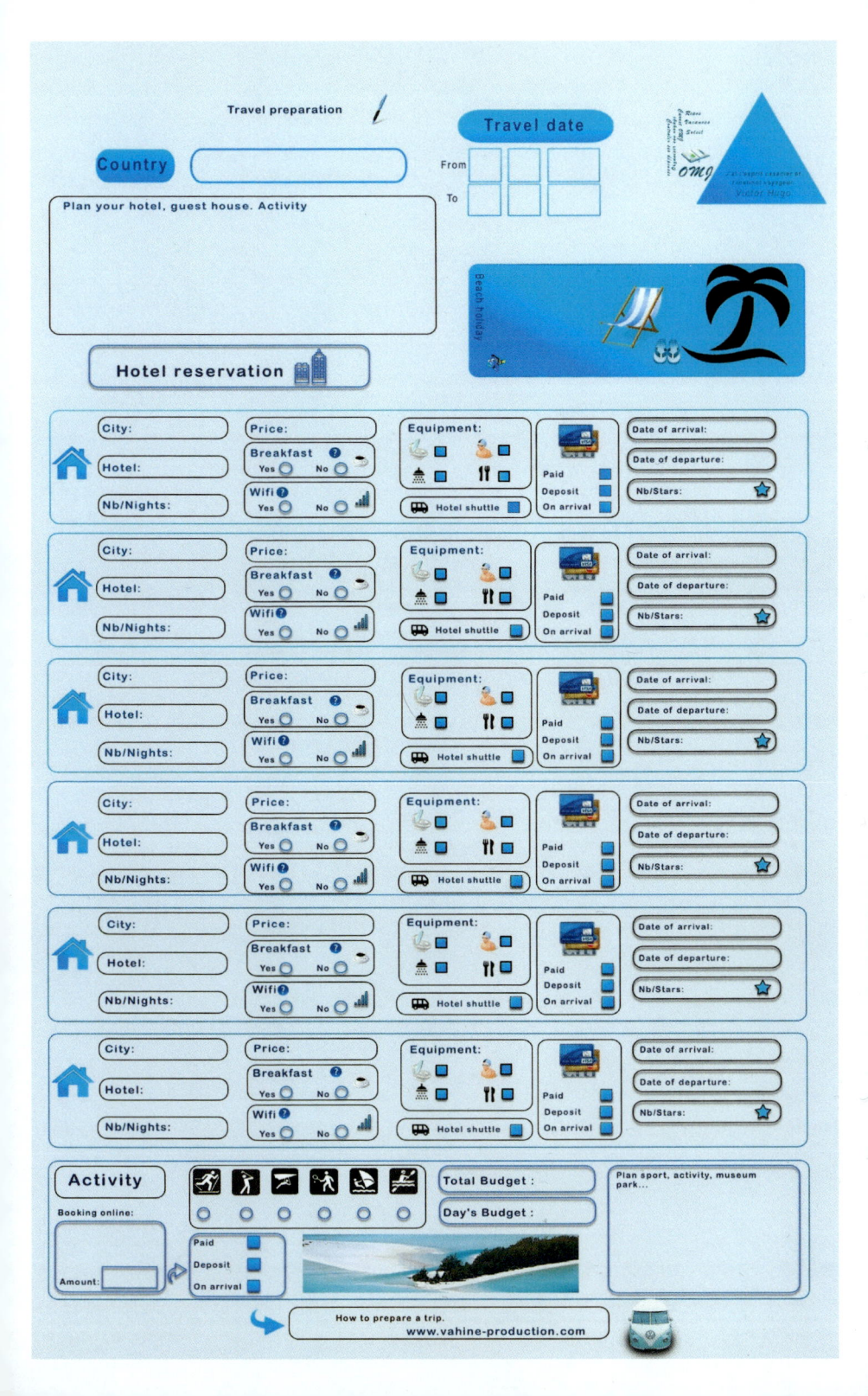

Country: _____

Travel date
From: □ □ □
To: □ □ □

Plan your hotel, guest house. Activity
_____

Beach holiday

Hotel reservation

Entry 1
- City:
- Hotel:
- Nb/Nights:
- Price:
- Breakfast: Yes ○ No ○
- Wifi: Yes ○ No ○
- Equipment: □ □ □ □ □
- Hotel shuttle □
- Paid □
- Deposit □
- On arrival □
- Date of arrival:
- Date of departure:
- Nb/Stars:

Entry 2
- City:
- Hotel:
- Nb/Nights:
- Price:
- Breakfast: Yes ○ No ○
- Wifi: Yes ○ No ○
- Equipment: □ □ □ □ □
- Hotel shuttle □
- Paid □
- Deposit □
- On arrival □
- Date of arrival:
- Date of departure:
- Nb/Stars:

Entry 3
- City:
- Hotel:
- Nb/Nights:
- Price:
- Breakfast: Yes ○ No ○
- Wifi: Yes ○ No ○
- Equipment: □ □ □ □ □
- Hotel shuttle □
- Paid □
- Deposit □
- On arrival □
- Date of arrival:
- Date of departure:
- Nb/Stars:

Entry 4
- City:
- Hotel:
- Nb/Nights:
- Price:
- Breakfast: Yes ○ No ○
- Wifi: Yes ○ No ○
- Equipment: □ □ □ □ □
- Hotel shuttle □
- Paid □
- Deposit □
- On arrival □
- Date of arrival:
- Date of departure:
- Nb/Stars:

Entry 5
- City:
- Hotel:
- Nb/Nights:
- Price:
- Breakfast: Yes ○ No ○
- Wifi: Yes ○ No ○
- Equipment: □ □ □ □ □
- Hotel shuttle □
- Paid □
- Deposit □
- On arrival □
- Date of arrival:
- Date of departure:
- Nb/Stars:

Entry 6
- City:
- Hotel:
- Nb/Nights:
- Price:
- Breakfast: Yes ○ No ○
- Wifi: Yes ○ No ○
- Equipment: □ □ □ □ □
- Hotel shuttle □
- Paid □
- Deposit □
- On arrival □
- Date of arrival:
- Date of departure:
- Nb/Stars:

Activity

Booking online:

Amount: _____
- Paid □
- Deposit □
- On arrival □

Total Budget:
Day's Budget:

Plan sport, activity, museum park...

How to prepare a trip.
www.vahine-production.com

NOTE

NOTE

Country

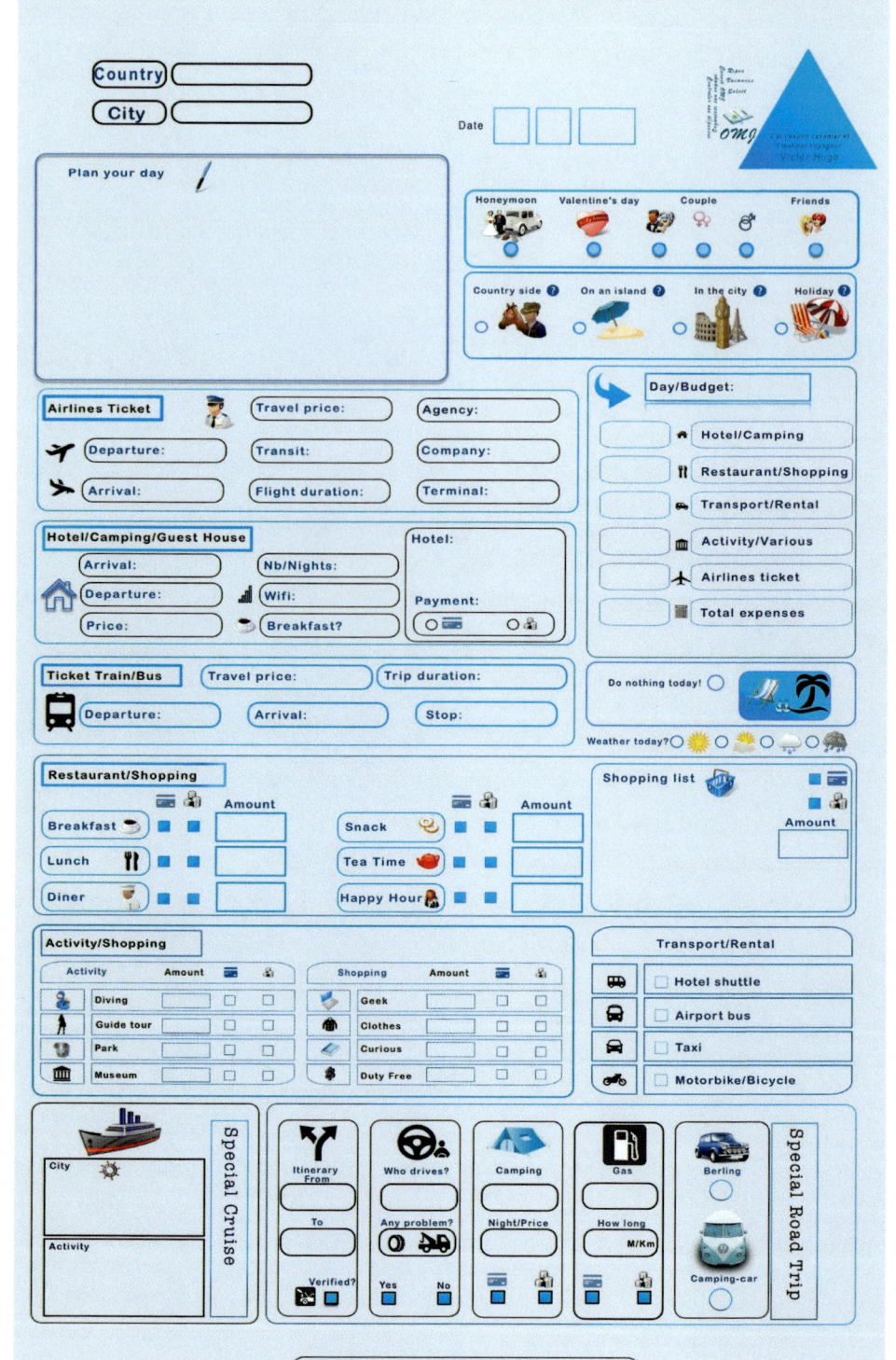

City

Date

Plan your day

Honeymoon   Valentine's day   Couple   Friends

Country side   On an island   In the city   Holiday

Airlines Ticket
- Departure:
- Arrival:
- Travel price:
- Transit:
- Flight duration:
- Agency:
- Company:
- Terminal:

Hotel/Camping/Guest House
- Arrival:
- Departure:
- Price:
- Nb/Nights:
- Wifi:
- Breakfast?
- Hotel:
- Payment:

Ticket Train/Bus
- Departure:
- Travel price:
- Arrival:
- Trip duration:
- Stop:

Day/Budget:
- Hotel/Camping
- Restaurant/Shopping
- Transport/Rental
- Activity/Various
- Airlines ticket
- Total expenses

Do nothing today!

Weather today?

Restaurant/Shopping
- Breakfast — Amount
- Lunch
- Diner
- Snack — Amount
- Tea Time
- Happy Hour

Shopping list — Amount

Activity/Shopping

Activity	Amount
Diving	
Guide tour	
Park	
Museum	

Shopping	Amount
Geek	
Clothes	
Curious	
Duty Free	

Transport/Rental
- Hotel shuttle
- Airport bus
- Taxi
- Motorbike/Bicycle

City

Activity

Special Cruise

- Itinerary From
- To
- Verified?
- Who drives?
- Any problem?
- Yes / No
- Camping
- Night/Price
- Gas
- How long M/Km
- Berling
- Camping-car

Special Road Trip

How to prepare a trip.
www.vahine-production.com

Note

Bali
Chili
Île de Pâques
Philippines
Mexique
Pérou
Brésil
Argentine
USA
Nouvelle-Zélande
Angleterre
Californie
Polynésie Française
Portugal
Singapour
Malaisie
France
Corée
Cambodge
Népal
Laos
Tibet
$
£
¥
€
Espagne
La Réunion
Hawaii
Les Antilles
Norvège
Thaïlande
Grèce
Chine
Inde
Seychelles
Madagascar
Belgique
Islande
Vietnam
Italie
Australie
Japon
Danemark
Allemagne
Roumanie
Guyane
Taïwan
Russie
Estonie
Suisse

French Touch

Country
City

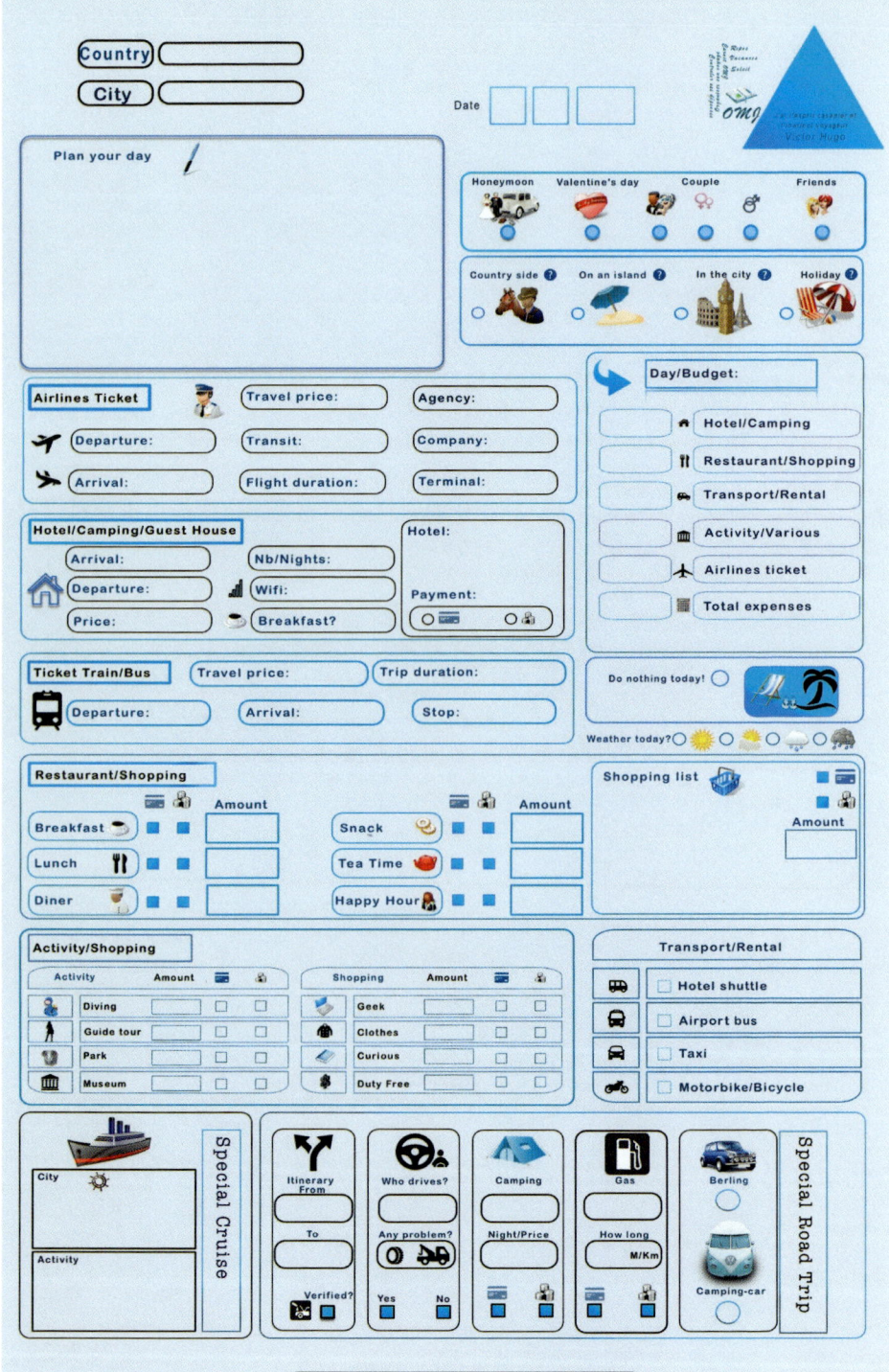

Date

Plan your day

Honeymoon Valentine's day Couple Friends

Country side On an island In the city Holiday

Airlines Ticket
- Travel price:
- Agency:
- Departure:
- Transit:
- Company:
- Arrival:
- Flight duration:
- Terminal:

Hotel/Camping/Guest House
- Arrival:
- Nb/Nights:
- Hotel:
- Departure:
- Wifi:
- Price:
- Breakfast?
- Payment:

Ticket Train/Bus
- Travel price:
- Trip duration:
- Departure:
- Arrival:
- Stop:

Day/Budget:
- Hotel/Camping
- Restaurant/Shopping
- Transport/Rental
- Activity/Various
- Airlines ticket
- Total expenses

Do nothing today!

Weather today?

Restaurant/Shopping
	Amount
Breakfast	
Lunch	
Diner	
Snack	
Tea Time	
Happy Hour	

Shopping list
Amount

Activity/Shopping
Activity	Amount
Diving	
Guide tour	
Park	
Museum	

Shopping	Amount
Geek	
Clothes	
Curious	
Duty Free	

Transport/Rental
- Hotel shuttle
- Airport bus
- Taxi
- Motorbike/Bicycle

Special Cruise
- City
- Activity

- Itinerary From
- To
- Verified?

- Who drives?
- Any problem?
- Yes No

- Camping
- Night/Price

- Gas
- How long M/Km

Special Road Trip
- Berling
- Camping-car

How to prepare a trip.
www.vahine-production.com

Note

Bali
Chili
Philippines Mexique
Île de Pâques Pérou
Brésil
Argentine
USA
Nouvelle-Zélande
Angleterre
Californie
Polynésie Française
Portugal
France
Singapour Corée
Cambodge
Malaisie Népal
Laos
Tibet
Espagne
La Réunion
Hawaii
Les Antilles
Norvège
Thaïlande
Grèce Chine Inde
Seychelles
Madagascar
Belgique
Islande
Vietnam
Italie
Australie
Japon
Danemark
Allemagne Guyane
Roumanie Taïwan
Russie
Estonie
Suisse

French Touch

Travel Planner

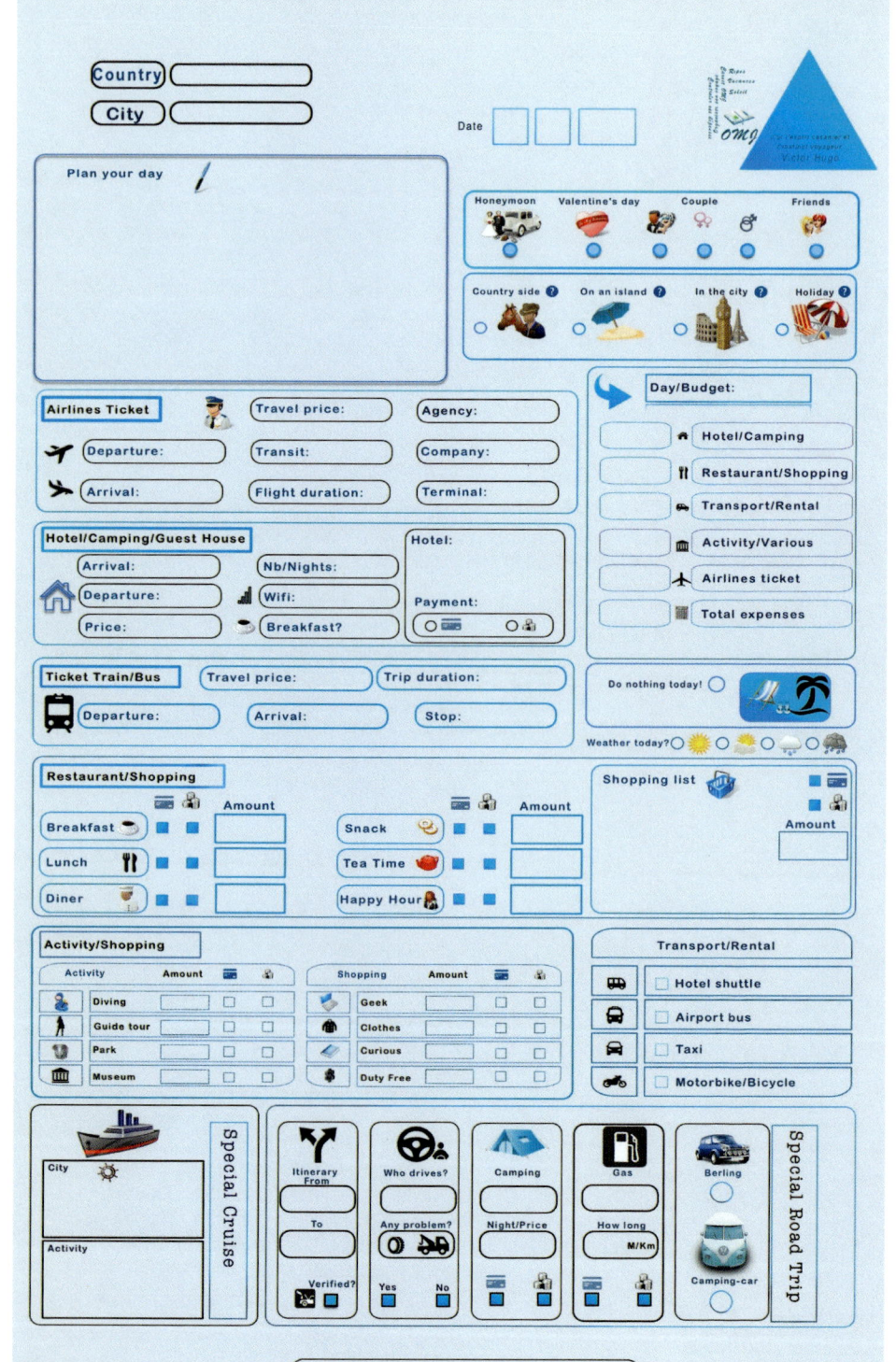

Country: _____
City: _____
Date: __ __ __

Plan your day

- Honeymoon
- Valentine's day
- Couple
- Friends

- Country side ?
- On an island ?
- In the city ?
- Holiday ?

Airlines Ticket
- Departure:
- Arrival:
- Travel price:
- Transit:
- Flight duration:
- Agency:
- Company:
- Terminal:

Day/Budget:
- Hotel/Camping
- Restaurant/Shopping
- Transport/Rental
- Activity/Various
- Airlines ticket
- Total expenses

Hotel/Camping/Guest House
- Arrival:
- Departure:
- Price:
- Nb/Nights:
- Wifi:
- Breakfast?
- Hotel:
- Payment:

Do nothing today!

Ticket Train/Bus
- Departure:
- Travel price:
- Arrival:
- Trip duration:
- Stop:

Weather today?

Restaurant/Shopping
	Amount			Amount
Breakfast		Snack		
Lunch		Tea Time		
Diner		Happy Hour		

Shopping list
Amount

Activity/Shopping

Activity	Amount		Shopping	Amount	
Diving			Geek		
Guide tour			Clothes		
Park			Curious		
Museum			Duty Free		

Transport/Rental
- Hotel shuttle
- Airport bus
- Taxi
- Motorbike/Bicycle

Special Cruise
- City
- Activity

- Itinerary From
- To
- Verified?
- Who drives?
- Any problem?
- Yes / No
- Camping
- Night/Price
- Gas
- How long M/Km
- Berling
- Camping-car

Special Road Trip

How to prepare a trip.
www.vahine-production.com

Note

Bali
Chili
Mexique
Pérou
Brésil
Argentine
USA
Île de Pâques
Philippines
Nouvelle-Zélande
Angleterre
Californie
Polynésie Française
Portugal
France
Corée
Cambodge
Singapour
Malaisie
Népal
Laos
Tibet
Espagne
La Réunion
Hawaii
Les Antilles
Norvège
Thaïlande
Grèce
Chine
Inde
Seychelles
Madagascar
Belgique
Islande
Vietnam
Italie
Australie
Japon
Danemark
Allemagne
Roumanie
Guyane
Taïwan
Russie
Estonie
Suisse

French Touch

Country
City
Date

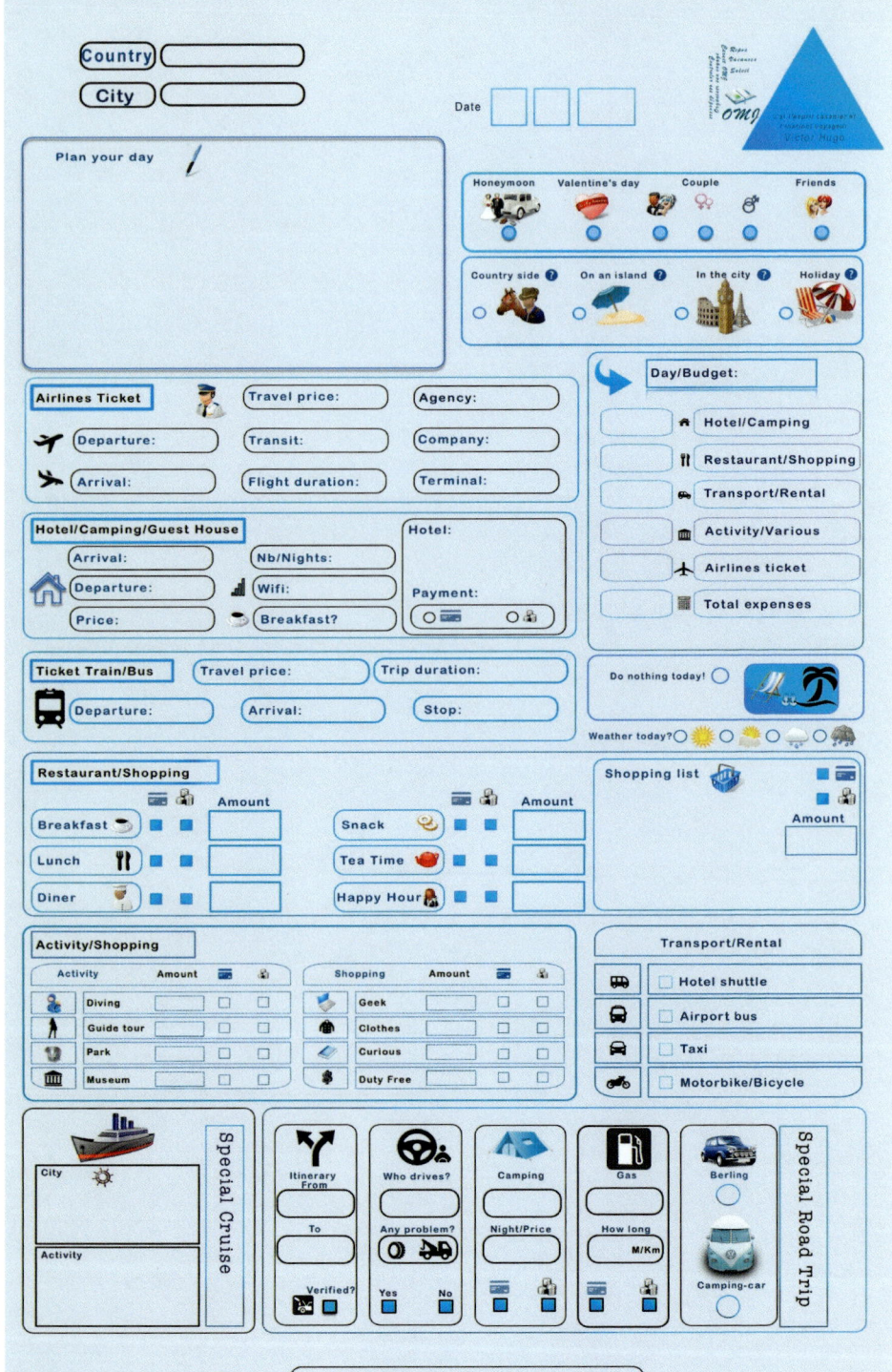

Plan your day

Honeymoon | Valentine's day | Couple | Friends

Country side | On an island | In the city | Holiday

Airlines Ticket
- Travel price:
- Agency:
- Departure:
- Transit:
- Company:
- Arrival:
- Flight duration:
- Terminal:

Hotel/Camping/Guest House
- Arrival:
- Nb/Nights:
- Hotel:
- Departure:
- Wifi:
- Price:
- Breakfast?
- Payment:

Ticket Train/Bus
- Travel price:
- Trip duration:
- Departure:
- Arrival:
- Stop:

Day/Budget:
- Hotel/Camping
- Restaurant/Shopping
- Transport/Rental
- Activity/Various
- Airlines ticket
- Total expenses

Do nothing today!

Weather today?

Restaurant/Shopping
Amount
- Breakfast
- Lunch
- Diner
- Snack
- Tea Time
- Happy Hour

Shopping list
Amount

Activity/Shopping

Activity | Amount
- Diving
- Guide tour
- Park
- Museum

Shopping | Amount
- Geek
- Clothes
- Curious
- Duty Free

Transport/Rental
- Hotel shuttle
- Airport bus
- Taxi
- Motorbike/Bicycle

Special Cruise
- City
- Activity

- Itinerary From
- To
- Verified?
- Who drives?
- Any problem?
- Yes / No
- Camping
- Night/Price
- Gas
- How long M/Km
- Berling
- Camping-car

Special Road Trip

How to prepare a trip.
www.vahine-production.com

Note

Bali
Chili
Philippines Mexique
Île de Pâques Perou
Bresil
Argentine
USA
Nouvelle-Zelande
Angleterre
Californie
Polynésie Française
Portugal
France
Corée
Singapour Cambodge
Malaisie Nepal
Laos
Tibet
Espagne
La Reunion
Hawaii
Les Antilles
Norvège
Thailande
Grèce Chine Inde
Seychelles
Madagascar
Belgique
Islande
Vietnam
Italie
Australie
Japon
Danemark
Allemagne Guyane
Roumanie Taiwan
Russie
Estonie
Suisse

French Touch

Country

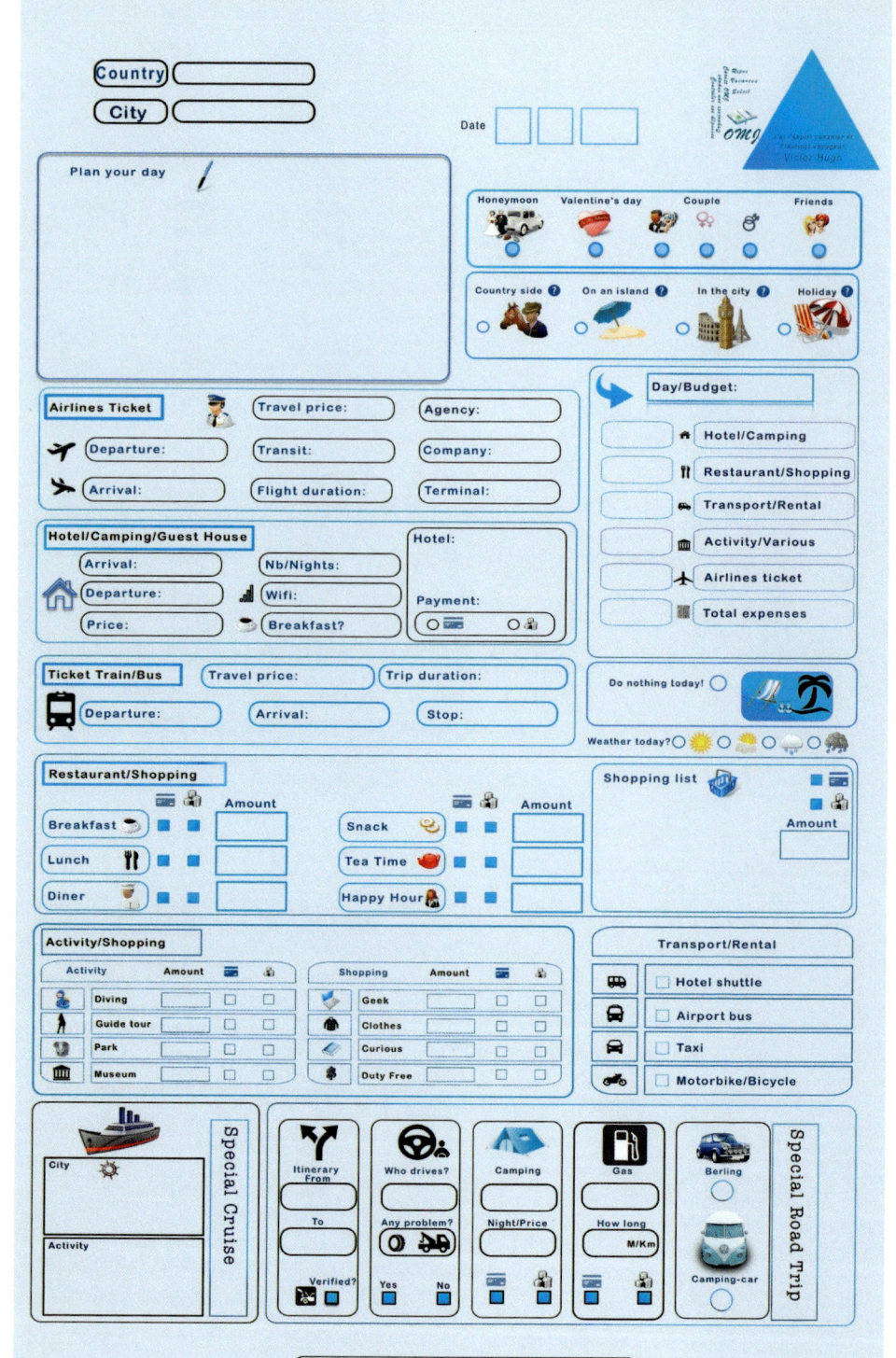

City

Date

Plan your day

Honeymoon   Valentine's day   Couple   Friends

Country side ?   On an island ?   In the city ?   Holiday ?

Airlines Ticket
- Travel price:
- Agency:
- Departure:
- Transit:
- Company:
- Arrival:
- Flight duration:
- Terminal:

Hotel/Camping/Guest House
- Arrival:
- Nb/Nights:
- Hotel:
- Departure:
- Wifi:
- Payment:
- Price:
- Breakfast?

Ticket Train/Bus
- Travel price:
- Trip duration:
- Departure:
- Arrival:
- Stop:

Day/Budget:
- Hotel/Camping
- Restaurant/Shopping
- Transport/Rental
- Activity/Various
- Airlines ticket
- Total expenses

Do nothing today!

Weather today?

Restaurant/Shopping

	Amount		Amount
Breakfast		Snack	
Lunch		Tea Time	
Diner		Happy Hour	

Shopping list

Amount

Activity/Shopping

Activity	Amount		Shopping	Amount	
Diving			Geek		
Guide tour			Clothes		
Park			Curious		
Museum			Duty Free		

Transport/Rental
- Hotel shuttle
- Airport bus
- Taxi
- Motorbike/Bicycle

City

Activity

Special Cruise

Itinerary From

To

Verified?

Who drives?

Any problem?

Yes   No

Camping

Night/Price

Gas

How long M/Km

Berling

Camping-car

Special Road Trip

How to prepare a trip.
www.vahine-production.com

Note

Bali
Chili
Mexique
Ile de Pâques
Philippines
Pérou
Brésil
Argentine
USA
Nouvelle-Zélande
Angleterre
Californie
Polynésie Française
Portugal
Singapour
France
Corée
Cambodge
Malaisie
Népal
Laos
Tibet
Espagne
La Reunion
Hawaii
Les Antilles
Norvège

Thailande
Grèce
Chine
Inde
Seychelles
Madagascar
Belgique
Islande
Vietnam
Italie
Australie
Japon
Danemark
Allemagne
Roumanie
Guyane
Taiwan
Russie
Estonie
Suisse

French Touch

Country
City
Date

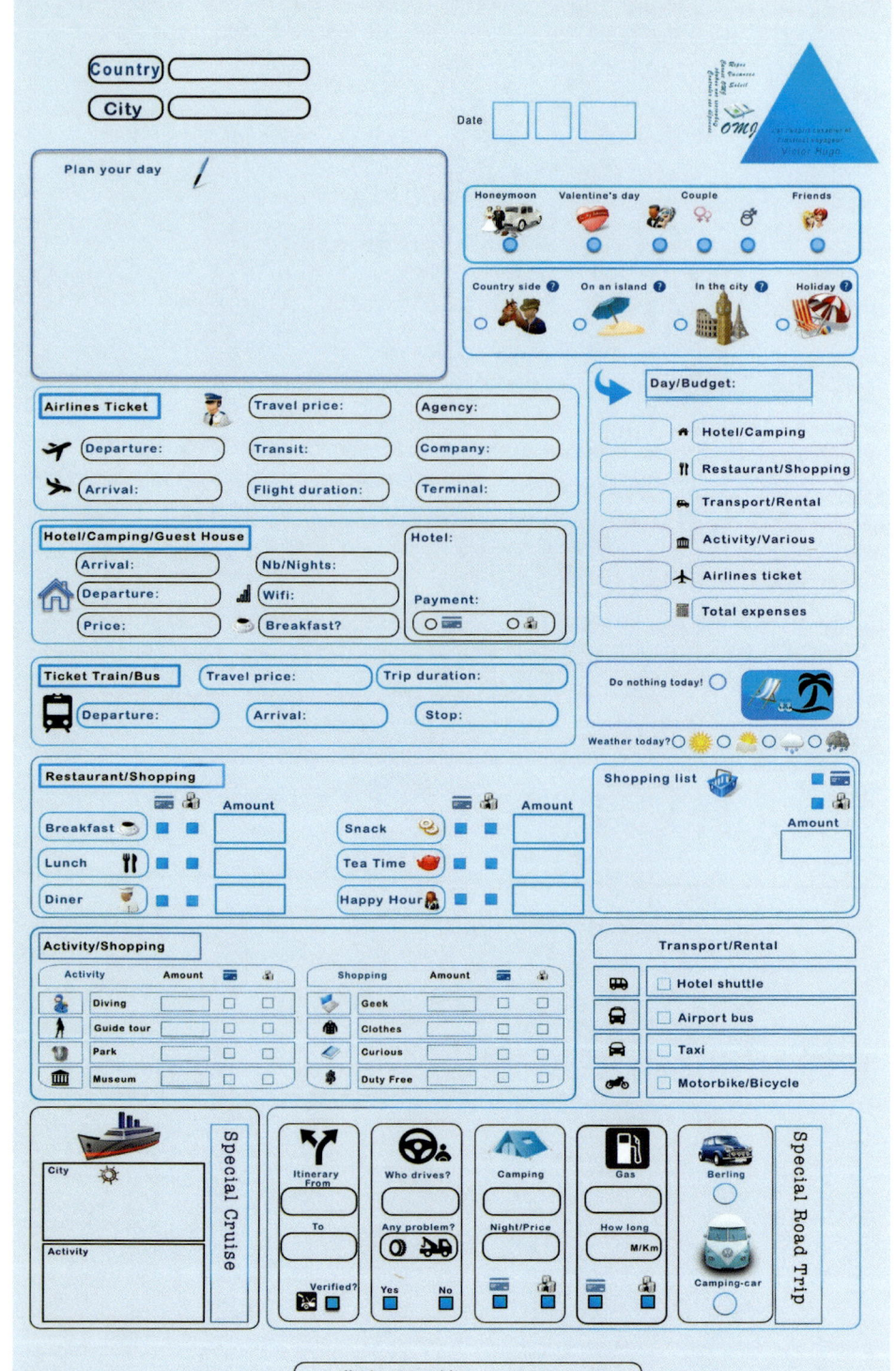

Plan your day

Honeymoon Valentine's day Couple Friends

Country side On an island In the city Holiday

Airlines Ticket
- Travel price:
- Agency:
- Departure:
- Transit:
- Company:
- Arrival:
- Flight duration:
- Terminal:

Hotel/Camping/Guest House
- Arrival:
- Nb/Nights:
- Hotel:
- Departure:
- Wifi:
- Price:
- Breakfast?
- Payment:

Ticket Train/Bus
- Travel price:
- Trip duration:
- Departure:
- Arrival:
- Stop:

Day/Budget:
- Hotel/Camping
- Restaurant/Shopping
- Transport/Rental
- Activity/Various
- Airlines ticket
- Total expenses

Do nothing today!

Weather today?

Restaurant/Shopping
- Breakfast — Amount
- Lunch
- Diner
- Snack
- Tea Time
- Happy Hour

Shopping list
Amount

Activity/Shopping

Activity	Amount
Diving	
Guide tour	
Park	
Museum	

Shopping	Amount
Geek	
Clothes	
Curious	
Duty Free	

Transport/Rental
- Hotel shuttle
- Airport bus
- Taxi
- Motorbike/Bicycle

Special Cruise
- City
- Activity

- Itinerary From
- To
- Verified?

- Who drives?
- Any problem?
- Yes No

- Camping
- Night/Price

- Gas
- How long M/Km

Special Road Trip
- Berling
- Camping-car

How to prepare a trip.
www.vahine-production.com

Note

Bali
Chili
Mexique
Pérou
Brésil
Argentine
USA
Île de Pâques
Philippines
Nouvelle-Zélande
Angleterre
Californie
Polynésie Française
Portugal
France
Corée
Cambodge
Singapour
Malaisie
Népal
Laos
Tibet
$
£
¥
€
Espagne
La Réunion
Hawaii
Les Antilles
Norvège
Thaïlande
Grèce
Chine
Inde
Seychelles
Madagascar
Belgique
Islande
Vietnam
Italie
Australie
Japon
Danemark
Allemagne
Roumanie
Guyane
Taïwan
Russie
Estonie
Suisse

French Touch

Country

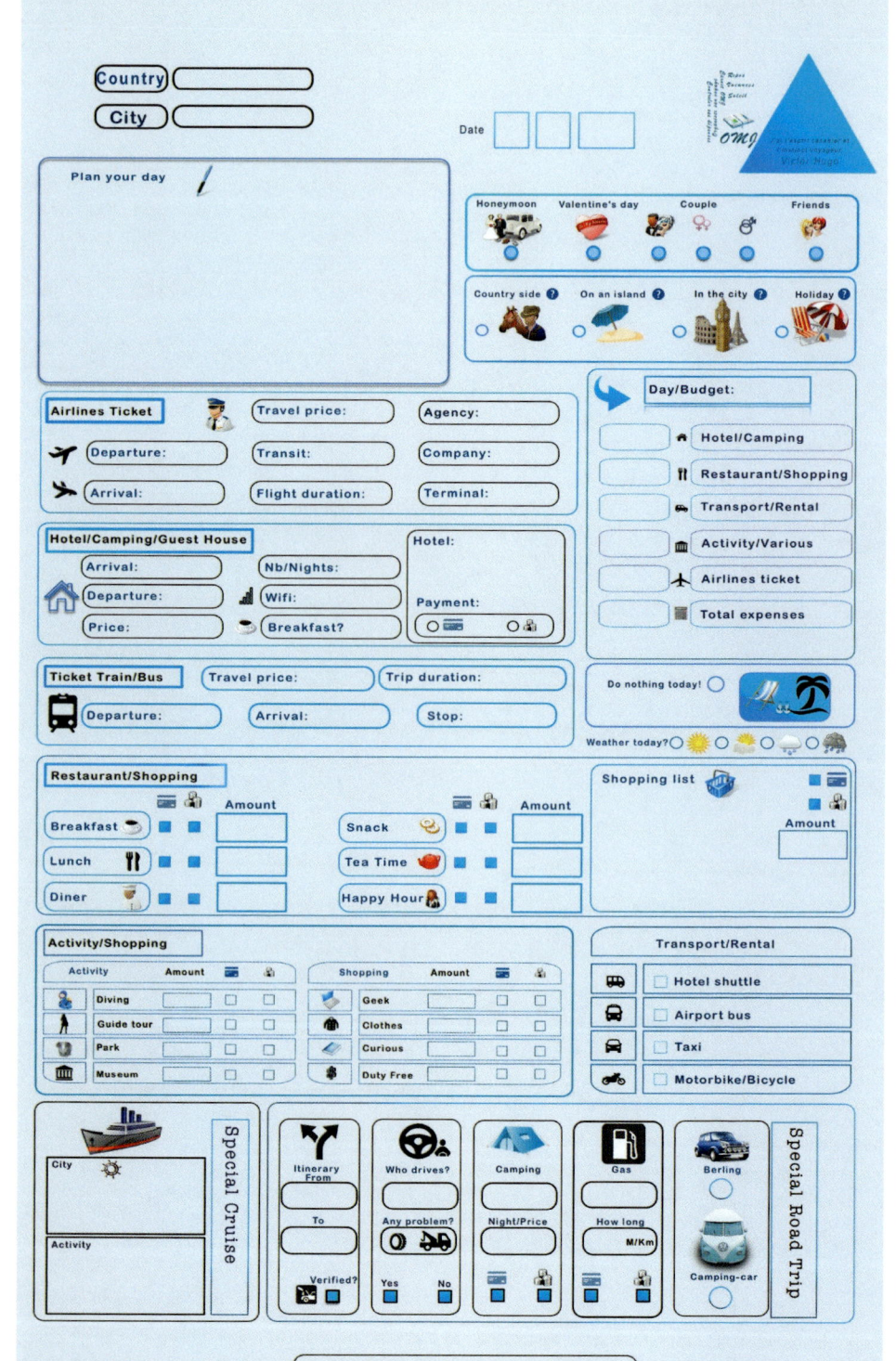

City

Date

Plan your day

Honeymoon | Valentine's day | Couple | Friends

Country side | On an island | In the city | Holiday

Airlines Ticket
- Travel price:
- Agency:
- Departure:
- Transit:
- Company:
- Arrival:
- Flight duration:
- Terminal:

Hotel/Camping/Guest House
- Arrival:
- Nb/Nights:
- Hotel:
- Departure:
- Wifi:
- Price:
- Breakfast?
- Payment:

Ticket Train/Bus
- Travel price:
- Trip duration:
- Departure:
- Arrival:
- Stop:

Day/Budget:
- Hotel/Camping
- Restaurant/Shopping
- Transport/Rental
- Activity/Various
- Airlines ticket
- Total expenses

Do nothing today!

Weather today?

Restaurant/Shopping
- Breakfast — Amount
- Lunch — Amount
- Diner — Amount
- Snack
- Tea Time
- Happy Hour

Shopping list — Amount

Activity/Shopping

Activity | Amount
- Diving
- Guide tour
- Park
- Museum

Shopping | Amount
- Geek
- Clothes
- Curious
- Duty Free

Transport/Rental
- Hotel shuttle
- Airport bus
- Taxi
- Motorbike/Bicycle

Special Cruise
- City
- Activity

Itinerary From / To
Who drives? / Any problem?
Camping / Night/Price
Gas / How long M/Km
Verified? Yes No

Special Road Trip
- Berling
- Camping-car

How to prepare a trip.
www.vahine-production.com

Note

Bali
Chili
Philippines
Île de Pâques
Mexique
Pérou
Brésil
Argentine
USA
Nouvelle-Zélande
Angleterre
Californie
Polynésie Française
Portugal
France
Corée
Singapour
Cambodge
Malaisie
Népal
Laos
Tibet
$ £ ¥ €
Espagne
La Réunion
Hawaii
Les Antilles
Norvège

Thaïlande
Grèce Chine
Inde
Seychelles
Madagascar
Belgique
Islande
Vietnam
Italie
Australie
Japon
Danemark
Allemagne
Roumanie
Guyane
Taïwan
Russie
Estonie
Suisse

French Touch

Country
City

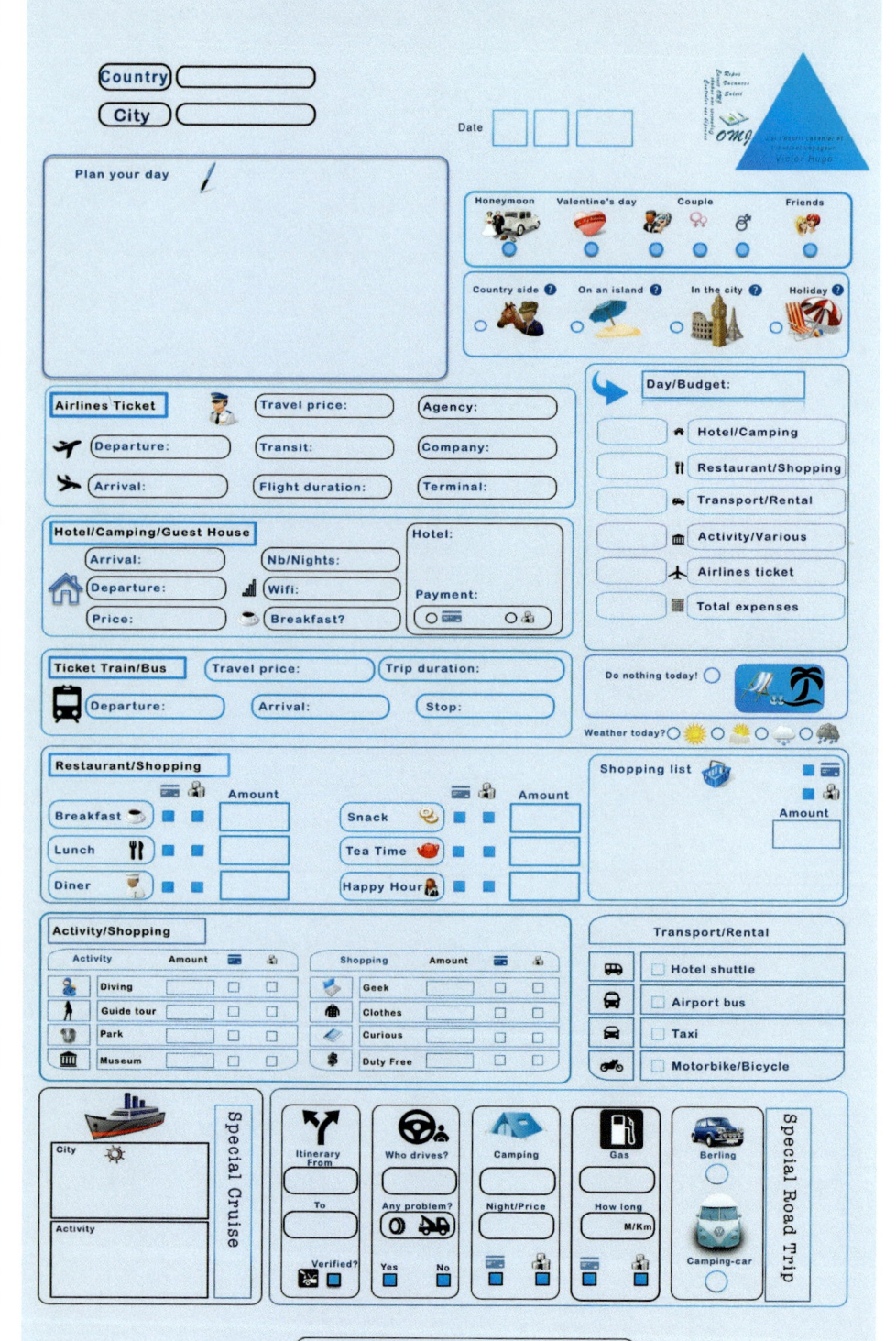

Date

Plan your day

Honeymoon Valentine's day Couple Friends

Country side On an island In the city Holiday

Day/Budget:
- Hotel/Camping
- Restaurant/Shopping
- Transport/Rental
- Activity/Various
- Airlines ticket
- Total expenses

Airlines Ticket
- Departure:
- Arrival:
- Travel price:
- Transit:
- Flight duration:
- Agency:
- Company:
- Terminal:

Hotel/Camping/Guest House
- Arrival:
- Departure:
- Price:
- Nb/Nights:
- Wifi:
- Breakfast?
- Hotel:
- Payment:

Ticket Train/Bus
- Departure:
- Travel price:
- Arrival:
- Trip duration:
- Stop:

Do nothing today!

Weather today?

Restaurant/Shopping
	Amount			Amount
Breakfast		Snack		
Lunch		Tea Time		
Diner		Happy Hour		

Shopping list

Amount

Activity/Shopping
Activity	Amount		Shopping	Amount	
Diving			Geek		
Guide tour			Clothes		
Park			Curious		
Museum			Duty Free		

Transport/Rental
- Hotel shuttle
- Airport bus
- Taxi
- Motorbike/Bicycle

Special Cruise
- City
- Activity

- Itinerary From
- To
- Verified?
- Who drives?
- Any problem?
- Yes / No
- Camping
- Night/Price
- Gas
- How long M/Km

Special Road Trip
- Berling
- Camping-car

How to prepare a trip.
www.vahine-production.com

Note

Bali
Chili
Mexique
Île des Philippines
Perou
Bresil
Argentine
USA
Nouvelle-Zelande
Angleterre
Californie
Polynésie Française
Portugal
France
Corée
Singapour
Cambodge
$
Nepal
£
Malaisie
Laos
¥
Tibet
€
Espagne
La Reunion
Hawaii
Les Antilles
Norvège

Thailande
Grèce
Chine
Inde
Seychelles
Madagascar
Belgique
Islande
Vietnam
Italie
Australie
Japon
Danemark
Guyane
Allemagne
Taiwan
Roumanie
Russie
Estonie
Suisse

French Touch

Country

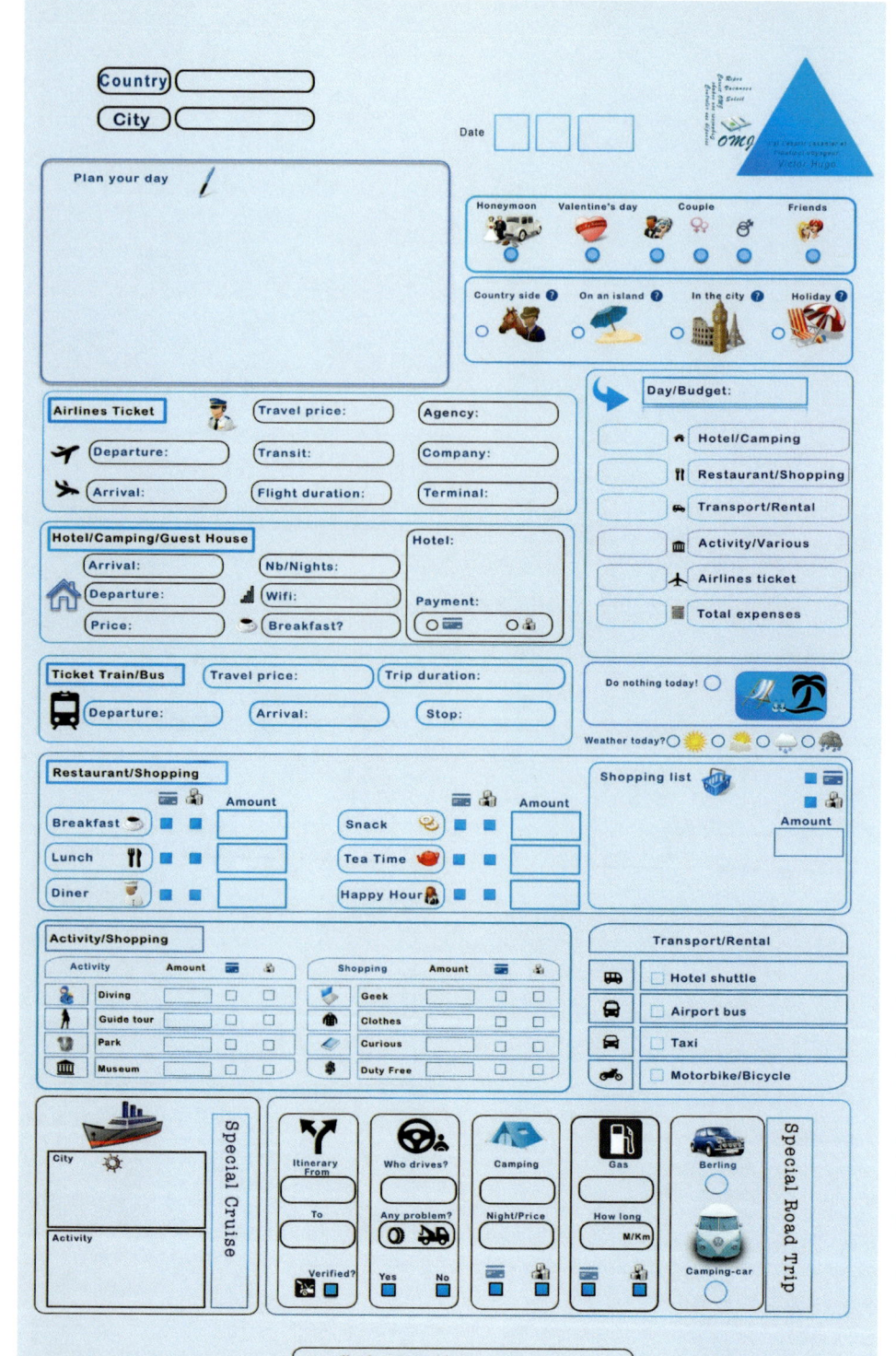

City

Date

Plan your day

Honeymoon • Valentine's day • Couple • Friends

Country side • On an island • In the city • Holiday

Airlines Ticket
- Departure:
- Arrival:
- Travel price:
- Transit:
- Flight duration:
- Agency:
- Company:
- Terminal:

Hotel/Camping/Guest House
- Arrival:
- Departure:
- Price:
- Nb/Nights:
- Wifi:
- Breakfast?
- Hotel:
- Payment:

Ticket Train/Bus
- Departure:
- Travel price:
- Arrival:
- Trip duration:
- Stop:

Day/Budget:
- Hotel/Camping
- Restaurant/Shopping
- Transport/Rental
- Activity/Various
- Airlines ticket
- Total expenses

Do nothing today!

Weather today?

Restaurant/Shopping
- Breakfast — Amount
- Lunch
- Diner
- Snack
- Tea Time
- Happy Hour

Shopping list — Amount

Activity/Shopping

Activity — Amount
- Diving
- Guide tour
- Park
- Museum

Shopping — Amount
- Geek
- Clothes
- Curious
- Duty Free

Transport/Rental
- Hotel shuttle
- Airport bus
- Taxi
- Motorbike/Bicycle

Special Cruise
- City
- Activity

- Itinerary From
- To
- Verified?
- Who drives?
- Any problem?
- Yes / No
- Camping
- Night/Price
- Gas
- How long M/Km

Special Road Trip
- Berling
- Camping-car

How to prepare a trip.
www.vahine-production.com

Note

Bali
Philippines
Île de Pâques
Chili
Mexique
Perou
Bresil
Argentine
USA
Nouvelle-Zelande
Angleterre
Californie
Polynésie Française
Portugal
Singapour
France
Corée
Cambodge
Malaisie
Nepal
Laos
Tibet
Espagne
La Reunion
Hawaii
Les Antilles
Norvège
Thailande
Grèce
Chine
Inde
Seychelles
Madagascar
Belgique
Islande
Vietnam
Italie
Australie
Japon
Danemark
Allemagne
Roumanie
Guyane
Taiwan
Russie
Estonie
Suisse

French Touch

Country

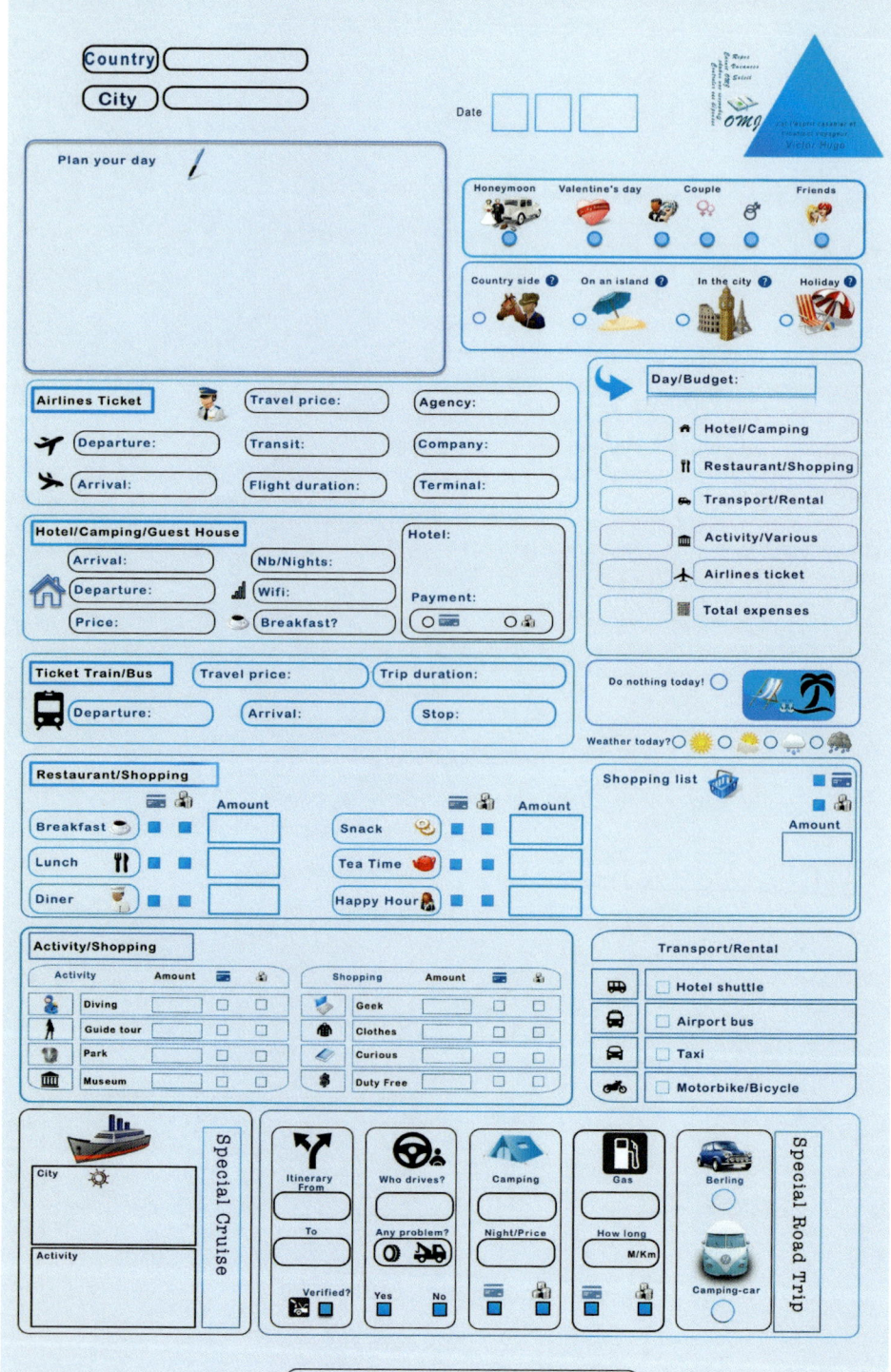

City

Date

Plan your day

Honeymoon · Valentine's day · Couple · Friends

Country side · On an island · In the city · Holiday

Airlines Ticket
- Departure:
- Arrival:
- Travel price:
- Transit:
- Flight duration:
- Agency:
- Company:
- Terminal:

Hotel/Camping/Guest House
- Arrival:
- Departure:
- Price:
- Nb/Nights:
- Wifi:
- Breakfast?
- Hotel:
- Payment:

Day/Budget:
- Hotel/Camping
- Restaurant/Shopping
- Transport/Rental
- Activity/Various
- Airlines ticket
- Total expenses

Ticket Train/Bus
- Departure:
- Travel price:
- Arrival:
- Trip duration:
- Stop:

Do nothing today!

Weather today?

Restaurant/Shopping
	Amount		Amount
Breakfast		Snack	
Lunch		Tea Time	
Diner		Happy Hour	

Shopping list

Amount

Activity/Shopping
Activity	Amount		Shopping	Amount	
Diving			Geek		
Guide tour			Clothes		
Park			Curious		
Museum			Duty Free		

Transport/Rental
- Hotel shuttle
- Airport bus
- Taxi
- Motorbike/Bicycle

Special Cruise
- City
- Activity

- Itinerary From
- To
- Verified?

- Who drives?
- Any problem?
- Yes / No

- Camping
- Night/Price

- Gas
- How long M/Km

Special Road Trip
- Berling
- Camping-car

How to prepare a trip.
www.vahine-production.com

Note

Bali
Chili
Philippines
Île de Pâques
Mexique
Perou
Bresil
Argentine
USA
Nouvelle-Zelande
Angleterre
Californie
Polynésie Française
Portugal
Singapour
Malaisie
France
Corée
Cambodge
Nepal
Laos
Tibet
Espagne
La Reunion
Hawaii
Les Antilles
Norvège

Thailande
Grèce
Chine
Inde
Seychelles
Madagascar
Belgique
Islande
Vietnam
Italie
Australie
Japon
Danemark
Allemagne
Roumanie
Guyane
Taiwan
Russie
Estonie
Suisse

French Touch

Country
City
Date

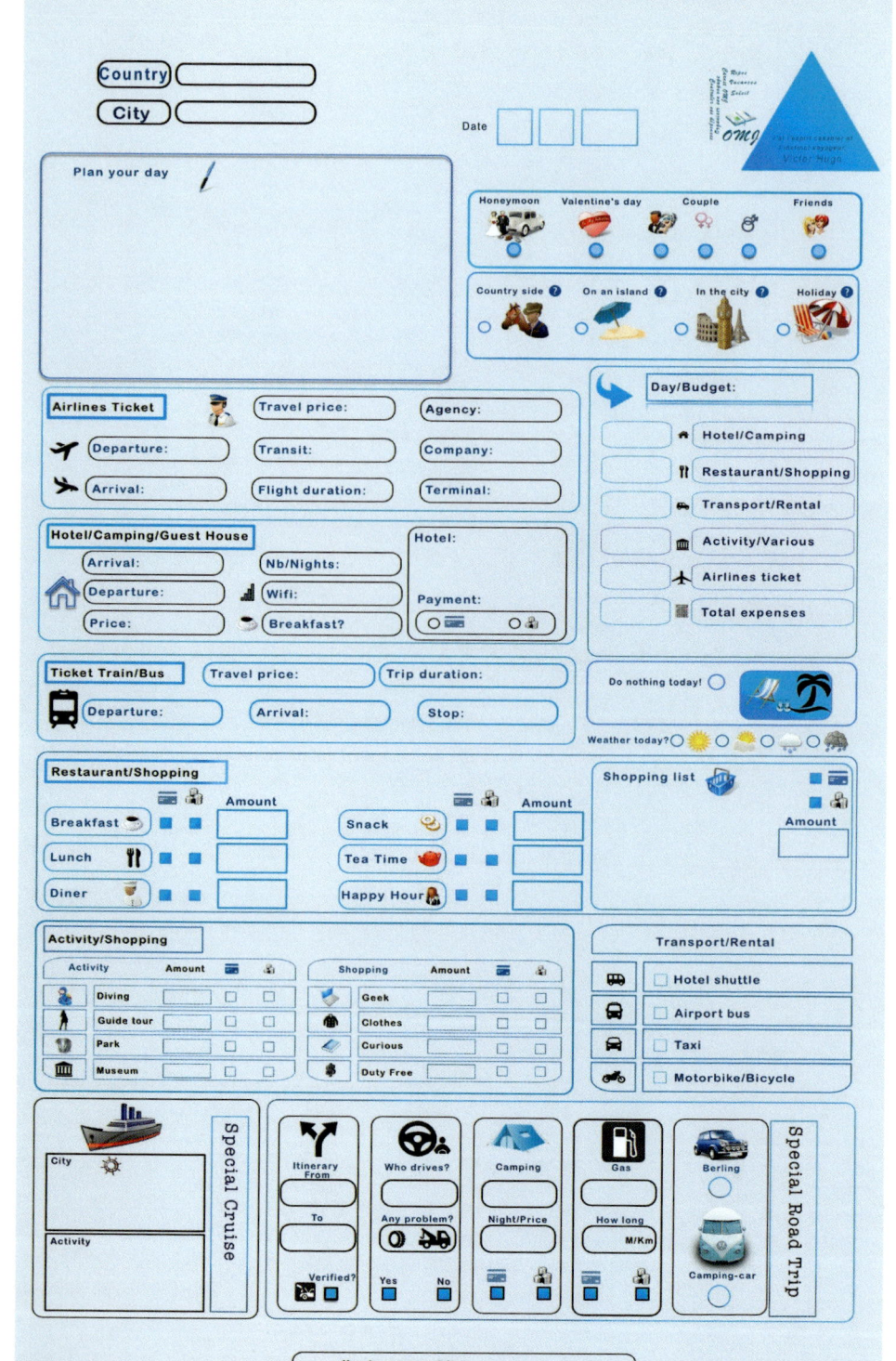

Plan your day

Honeymoon · Valentine's day · Couple · Friends

Country side · On an island · In the city · Holiday

Airlines Ticket
- Travel price:
- Agency:
- Departure:
- Transit:
- Company:
- Arrival:
- Flight duration:
- Terminal:

Hotel/Camping/Guest House
- Arrival:
- Nb/Nights:
- Hotel:
- Departure:
- Wifi:
- Payment:
- Price:
- Breakfast?

Ticket Train/Bus
- Travel price:
- Trip duration:
- Departure:
- Arrival:
- Stop:

Day/Budget:
- Hotel/Camping
- Restaurant/Shopping
- Transport/Rental
- Activity/Various
- Airlines ticket
- Total expenses

Do nothing today!

Weather today?

Restaurant/Shopping
	Amount		Amount
Breakfast		Snack	
Lunch		Tea Time	
Diner		Happy Hour	

Shopping list
Amount

Activity/Shopping

Activity	Amount		Shopping	Amount	
Diving			Geek		
Guide tour			Clothes		
Park			Curious		
Museum			Duty Free		

Transport/Rental
- Hotel shuttle
- Airport bus
- Taxi
- Motorbike/Bicycle

Special Cruise
- City
- Activity

- Itinerary From
- To
- Verified?

- Who drives?
- Any problem?
- Yes / No

- Camping
- Night/Price

- Gas
- How long M/Km

Special Road Trip
- Berling
- Camping-car

How to prepare a trip.
www.vahine-production.com

Note

Bali
Philippines
Chili
Île de Pâques
Mexique
Pérou
Brésil
Argentine
USA
Nouvelle-Zélande
Angleterre
Californie
Polynésie Française
Portugal
Singapour
France
Corée
Cambodge
Malaisie
Nepal
Laos
Tibet
Espagne
La Reunion
Hawaii
Les Antilles
Norvège

Thaïlande
Grèce
Chine
Inde
Seychelles
Madagascar
Belgique
Islande
Vietnam
Italie
Australie
Japon
Danemark
Allemagne
Guyane
Roumanie
Taiwan
Russie
Estonie
Suisse

French Touch

Country / City

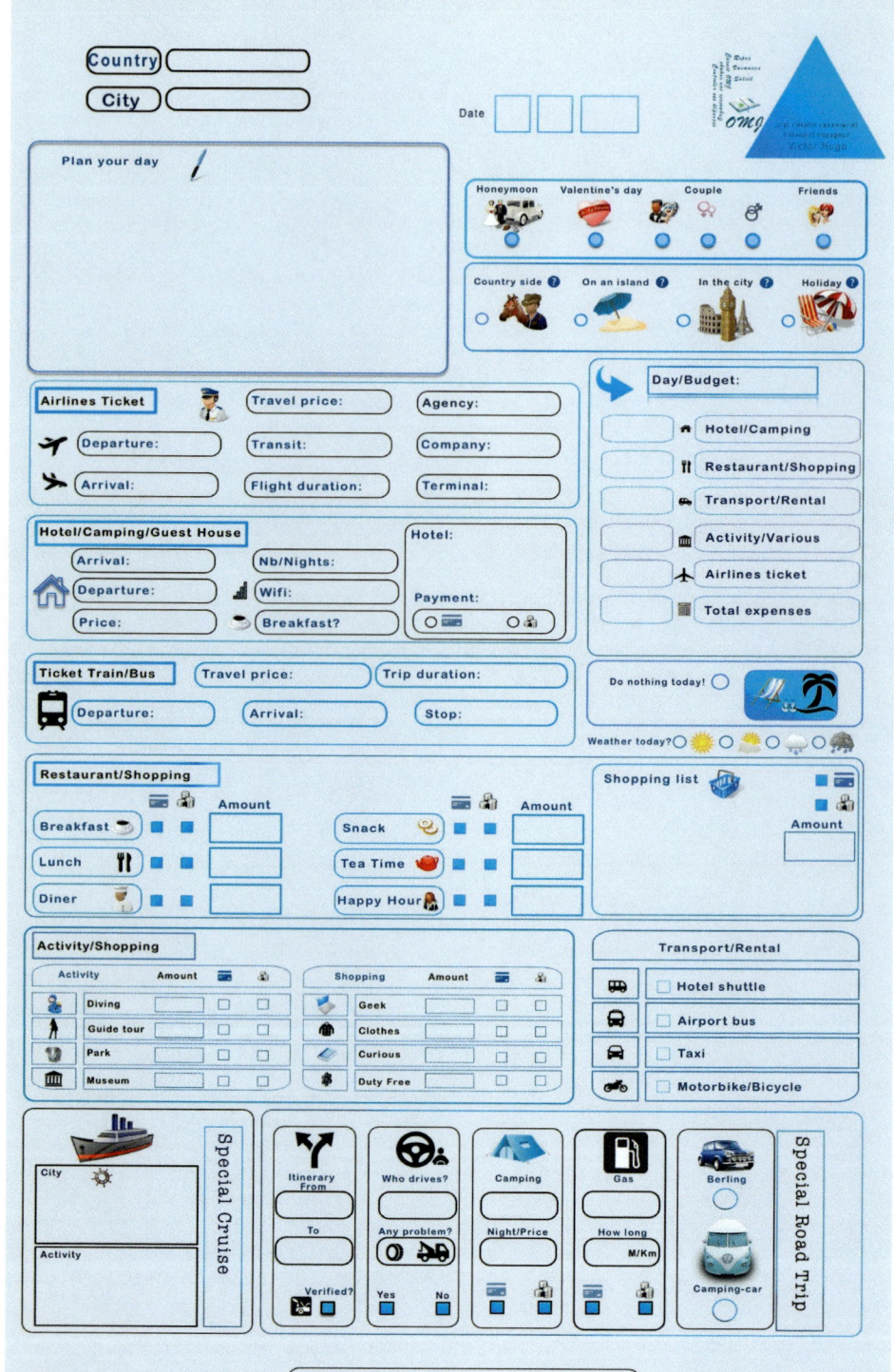

Date

Plan your day

Honeymoon | Valentine's day | Couple | Friends

Country side | On an island | In the city | Holiday

Airlines Ticket
- Travel price:
- Agency:
- Departure:
- Transit:
- Company:
- Arrival:
- Flight duration:
- Terminal:

Hotel/Camping/Guest House
- Arrival:
- Nb/Nights:
- Hotel:
- Departure:
- Wifi:
- Payment:
- Price:
- Breakfast?

Ticket Train/Bus
- Travel price:
- Trip duration:
- Departure:
- Arrival:
- Stop:

Day/Budget:
- Hotel/Camping
- Restaurant/Shopping
- Transport/Rental
- Activity/Various
- Airlines ticket
- Total expenses

Do nothing today!

Weather today?

Restaurant/Shopping
	Amount		Amount
Breakfast		Snack	
Lunch		Tea Time	
Diner		Happy Hour	

Shopping list — Amount

Activity/Shopping

Activity — Amount
- Diving
- Guide tour
- Park
- Museum

Shopping — Amount
- Geek
- Clothes
- Curious
- Duty Free

Transport/Rental
- Hotel shuttle
- Airport bus
- Taxi
- Motorbike/Bicycle

Special Cruise
- City
- Activity

- Itinerary From / To
- Verified?
- Who drives?
- Any problem? Yes / No
- Camping
- Night/Price
- Gas
- How long M/Km

Special Road Trip
- Berling
- Camping-car

How to prepare a trip.
www.vahine-production.com

Note

Bali
Chili
Philippines
Île de Pâques
Mexique
Perou
Bresil
Argentine
USA
Nouvelle-Zelande
Angleterre
Californie
Polynésie Française
Portugal
France
Corée
Singapour
Cambodge
Malaisie
Nepal
Laos
Tibet
$
£
¥
€
Espagne
La Reunion
Hawaii
Les Antilles
Norvège

Thailande
Grèce
Chine
Inde
Seychelles
Madagascar
Belgique
Islande
Vietnam
Italie
Australie
Japon
Danemark
Guyane
Taiwan
Allemagne
Roumanie
Russie
Estonie
Suisse

French Touch

Country
City
Date

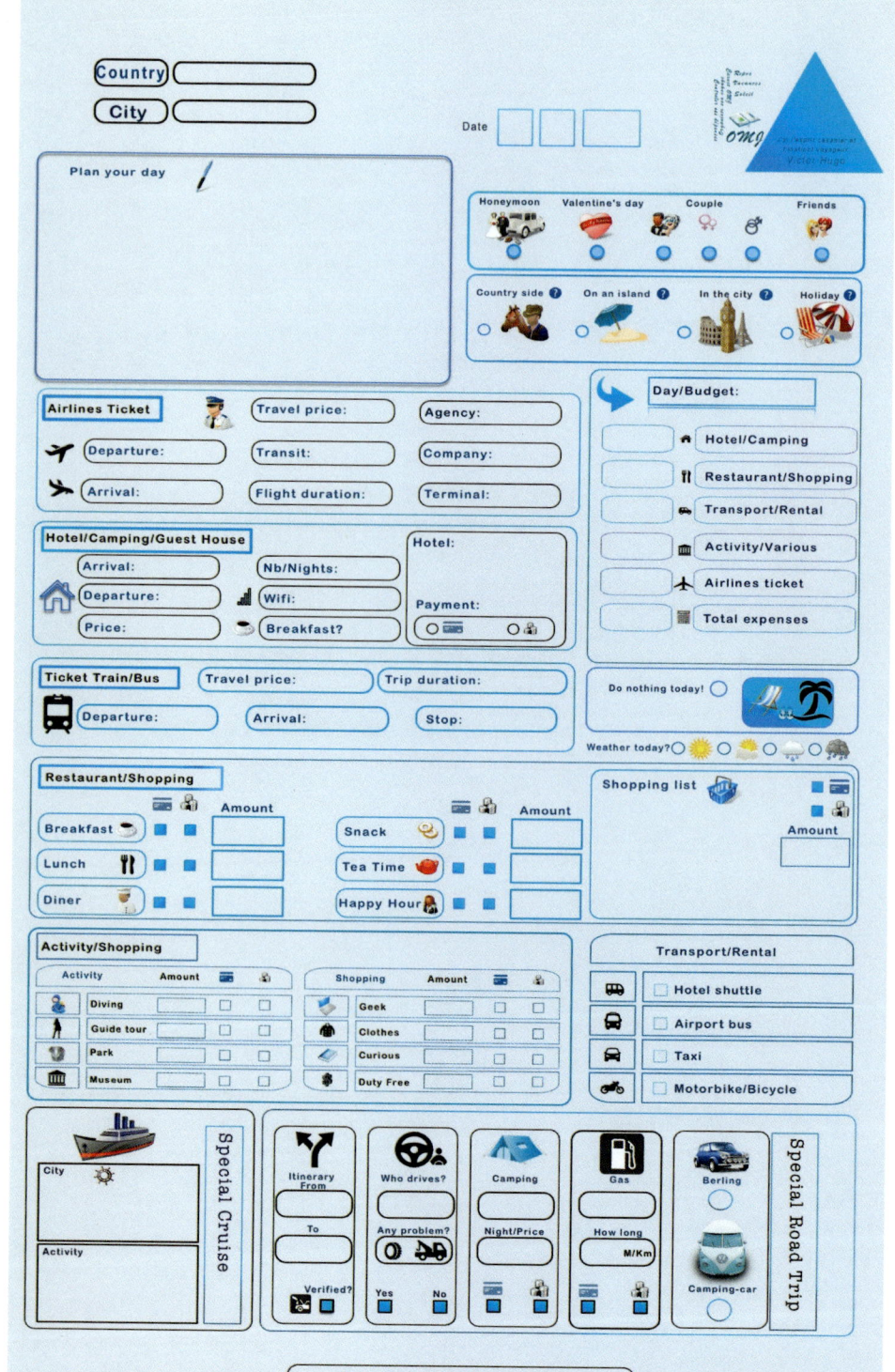

Plan your day

Honeymoon   Valentine's day   Couple   Friends

Country side   On an island   In the city   Holiday

Airlines Ticket
- Travel price:
- Agency:
- Departure:
- Transit:
- Company:
- Arrival:
- Flight duration:
- Terminal:

Day/Budget:
- Hotel/Camping
- Restaurant/Shopping
- Transport/Rental
- Activity/Various
- Airlines ticket
- Total expenses

Hotel/Camping/Guest House
- Arrival:
- Nb/Nights:
- Hotel:
- Departure:
- Wifi:
- Price:
- Breakfast?
- Payment:

Ticket Train/Bus
- Travel price:
- Trip duration:
- Departure:
- Arrival:
- Stop:

Do nothing today!

Weather today?

Restaurant/Shopping
	Amount		Amount
Breakfast		Snack	
Lunch		Tea Time	
Diner		Happy Hour	

Shopping list
Amount

Activity/Shopping
Activity	Amount		Shopping	Amount	
Diving			Geek		
Guide tour			Clothes		
Park			Curious		
Museum			Duty Free		

Transport/Rental
- Hotel shuttle
- Airport bus
- Taxi
- Motorbike/Bicycle

Special Cruise
- City
- Activity

Special Road Trip
- Itinerary From / To
- Verified?
- Who drives?
- Any problem? Yes / No
- Camping — Night/Price
- Gas — How long M/Km
- Berling
- Camping-car

How to prepare a trip.
www.vahine-production.com

Note

Bali
Chili
Philippines
Île de Pâques
Mexique
Perou
Brésil
Argentine
USA
Nouvelle-Zelande
Angleterre
Californie
Polynésie Française
Portugal
France
Corée
Singapour
Cambodge
Malaisie
Nepal
Laos
Tibet
Espagne
La Reunion
Hawaii
Les Antilles
Norvège

Thailande
Grèce
Chine
Inde
Seychelles
Madagascar
Belgique
Islande
Vietnam
Italie
Australie
Japon
Danemark
Allemagne
Guyane
Taïwan
Roumanie
Russie
Estonie
Suisse

French Touch

Country
City

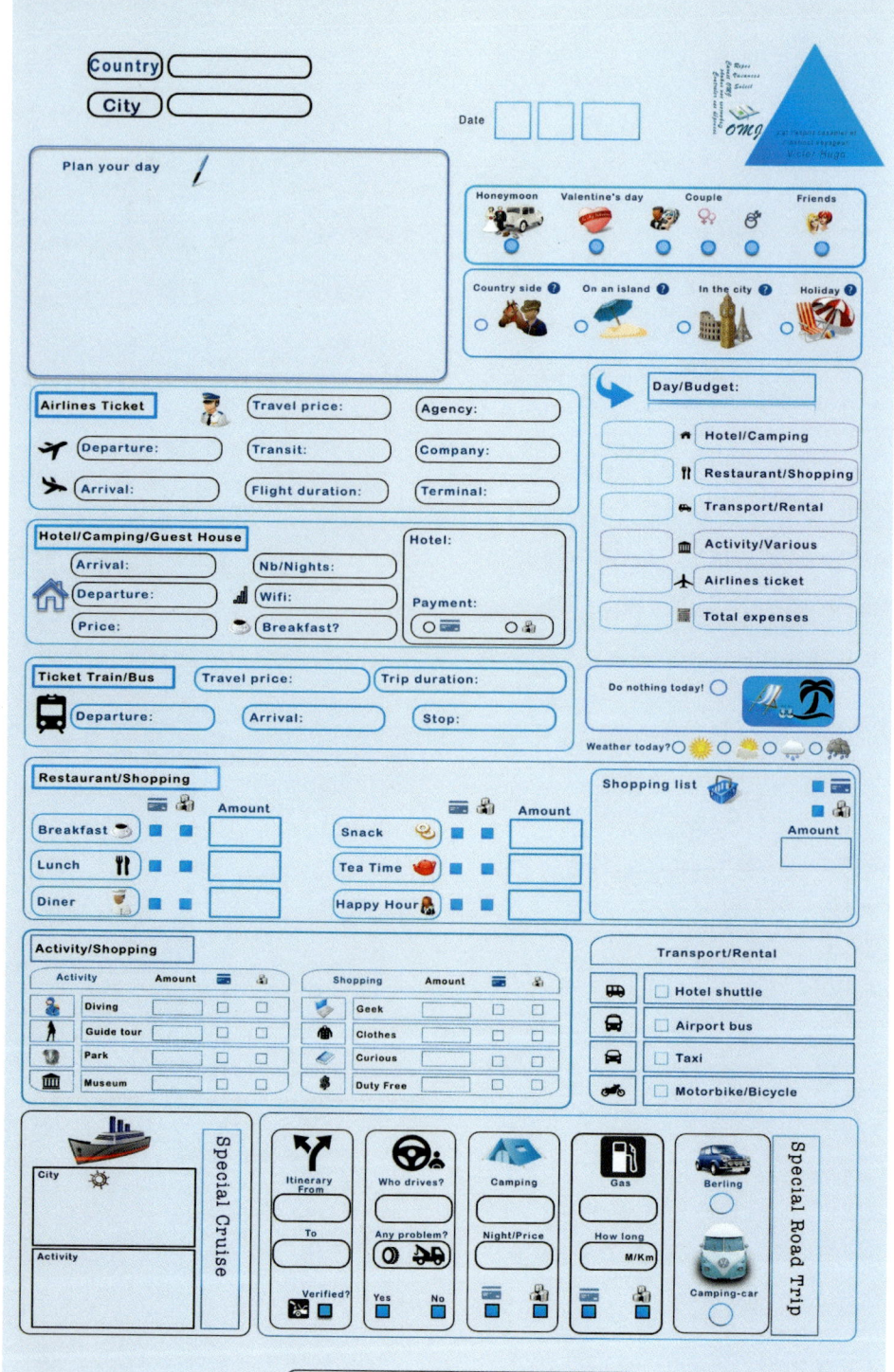

Date

Plan your day

Honeymoon | Valentine's day | Couple | Friends

Country side | On an island | In the city | Holiday

Airlines Ticket
- Travel price:
- Agency:
- Departure:
- Transit:
- Company:
- Arrival:
- Flight duration:
- Terminal:

Hotel/Camping/Guest House
- Hotel:
- Arrival:
- Nb/Nights:
- Departure:
- Wifi:
- Payment:
- Price:
- Breakfast?

Day/Budget:
- Hotel/Camping
- Restaurant/Shopping
- Transport/Rental
- Activity/Various
- Airlines ticket
- Total expenses

Ticket Train/Bus
- Travel price:
- Trip duration:
- Departure:
- Arrival:
- Stop:

Do nothing today!

Weather today?

Restaurant/Shopping
	Amount		Amount
Breakfast		Snack	
Lunch		Tea Time	
Diner		Happy Hour	

Shopping list
Amount

Activity/Shopping
Activity — Amount
- Diving
- Guide tour
- Park
- Museum

Shopping — Amount
- Geek
- Clothes
- Curious
- Duty Free

Transport/Rental
- Hotel shuttle
- Airport bus
- Taxi
- Motorbike/Bicycle

Special Cruise
- City
- Activity

- Itinerary From
- To
- Verified?

- Who drives?
- Any problem?
- Yes / No

- Camping
- Night/Price

- Gas
- How long M/Km

Special Road Trip
- Berling
- Camping-car

How to prepare a trip.
www.vahine-production.com

Note

Bali
Chili
Philippines
Île de Pâques
Mexique
Pérou
Brésil
Argentine
USA
Nouvelle-Zélande
Angleterre
Californie
Polynésie Française
Portugal
France
Corée
$
Cambodge
£
Singapour
Népal
Malaisie
Laos
¥
Tibet
€
Espagne
La Réunion
Hawaii
Les Antilles
Norvège

Thaïlande
Grèce Chine
Inde
Seychelles
Madagascar
Belgique
Islande
Vietnam
Italie
Australie
Japon
Danemark
Allemagne
Guyane
Roumanie
Taiwan
Russie
Estonie
Suisse

French Touch

Country

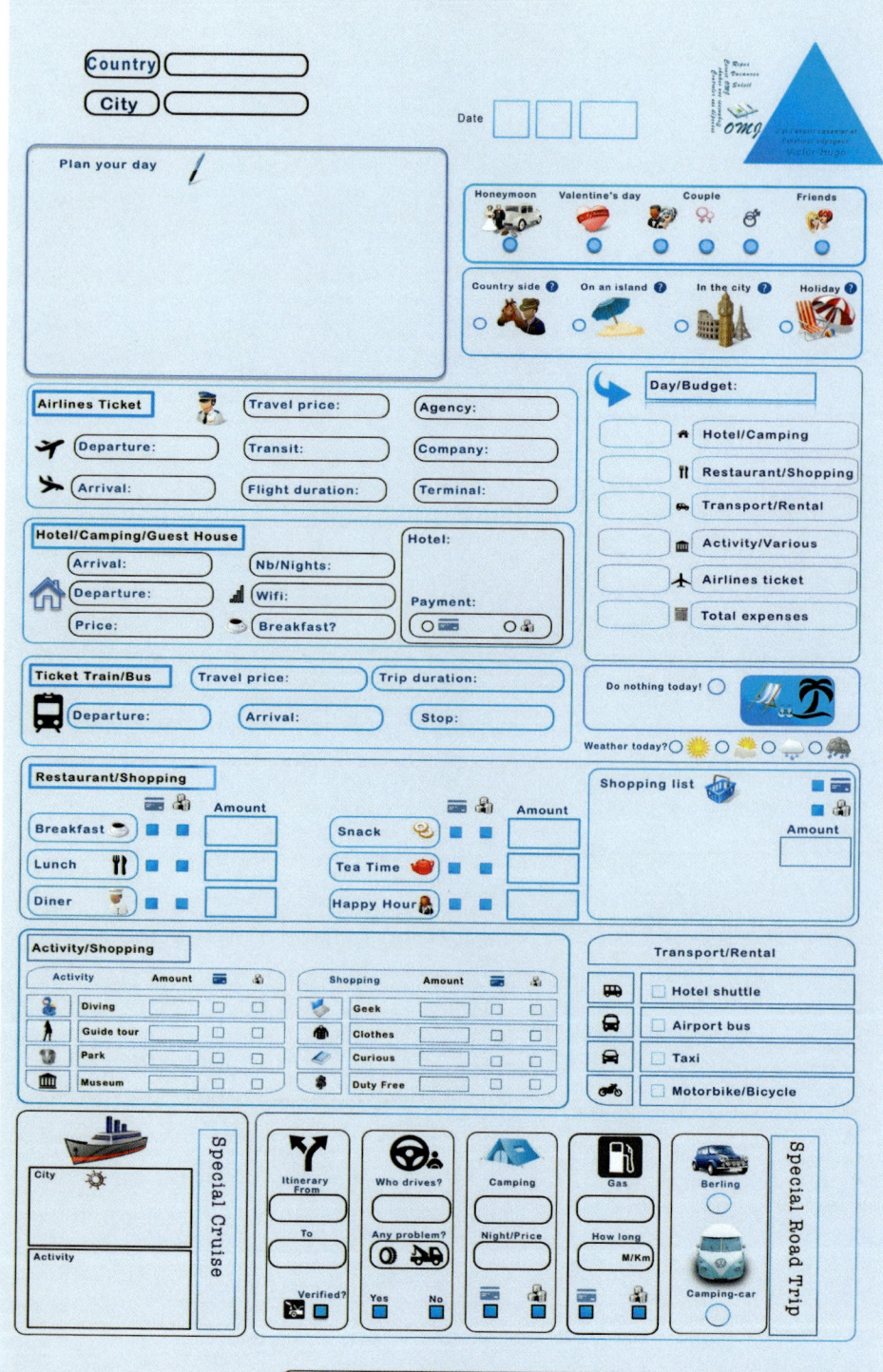

City

Date

Plan your day

Honeymoon   Valentine's day   Couple   Friends

Country side   On an island   In the city   Holiday

Airlines Ticket
- Departure:
- Arrival:
- Travel price:
- Transit:
- Flight duration:
- Agency:
- Company:
- Terminal:

Hotel/Camping/Guest House
- Arrival:
- Departure:
- Price:
- Nb/Nights:
- Wifi:
- Breakfast?
- Hotel:
- Payment:

Ticket Train/Bus
- Departure:
- Travel price:
- Arrival:
- Trip duration:
- Stop:

Day/Budget:
- Hotel/Camping
- Restaurant/Shopping
- Transport/Rental
- Activity/Various
- Airlines ticket
- Total expenses

Do nothing today!

Weather today?

Restaurant/Shopping
	Amount		Amount
Breakfast		Snack	
Lunch		Tea Time	
Diner		Happy Hour	

Shopping list
Amount

Activity/Shopping

Activity	Amount		Shopping	Amount	
Diving			Geek		
Guide tour			Clothes		
Park			Curious		
Museum			Duty Free		

Transport/Rental
- Hotel shuttle
- Airport bus
- Taxi
- Motorbike/Bicycle

Special Cruise
- City
- Activity

- Itinerary From
- To
- Verified?
- Who drives?
- Any problem?
- Yes / No
- Camping
- Night/Price
- Gas
- How long M/Km
- Berling
- Camping-car

Special Road Trip

How to prepare a trip.
www.vahine-production.com

Note

Bali
Chili
Mexique
Philippines
Ile de Pâques
Pérou
Brésil
Argentine
USA
Nouvelle-Zélande
Angleterre
Californie
Polynésie Française
Portugal
Singapour
France
Corée
Cambodge
Malaisie
Népal
Laos
Tibet
Espagne
La Réunion
Hawaii
Les Antilles
Norvège

Thaïlande
Grèce
Chine
Inde
Seychelles
Madagascar
Belgique
Islande
Vietnam
Italie
Australie
Japon
Danemark
Allemagne
Guyane
Roumanie
Taiwan
Russie
Estonie
Suisse

French Touch

Country

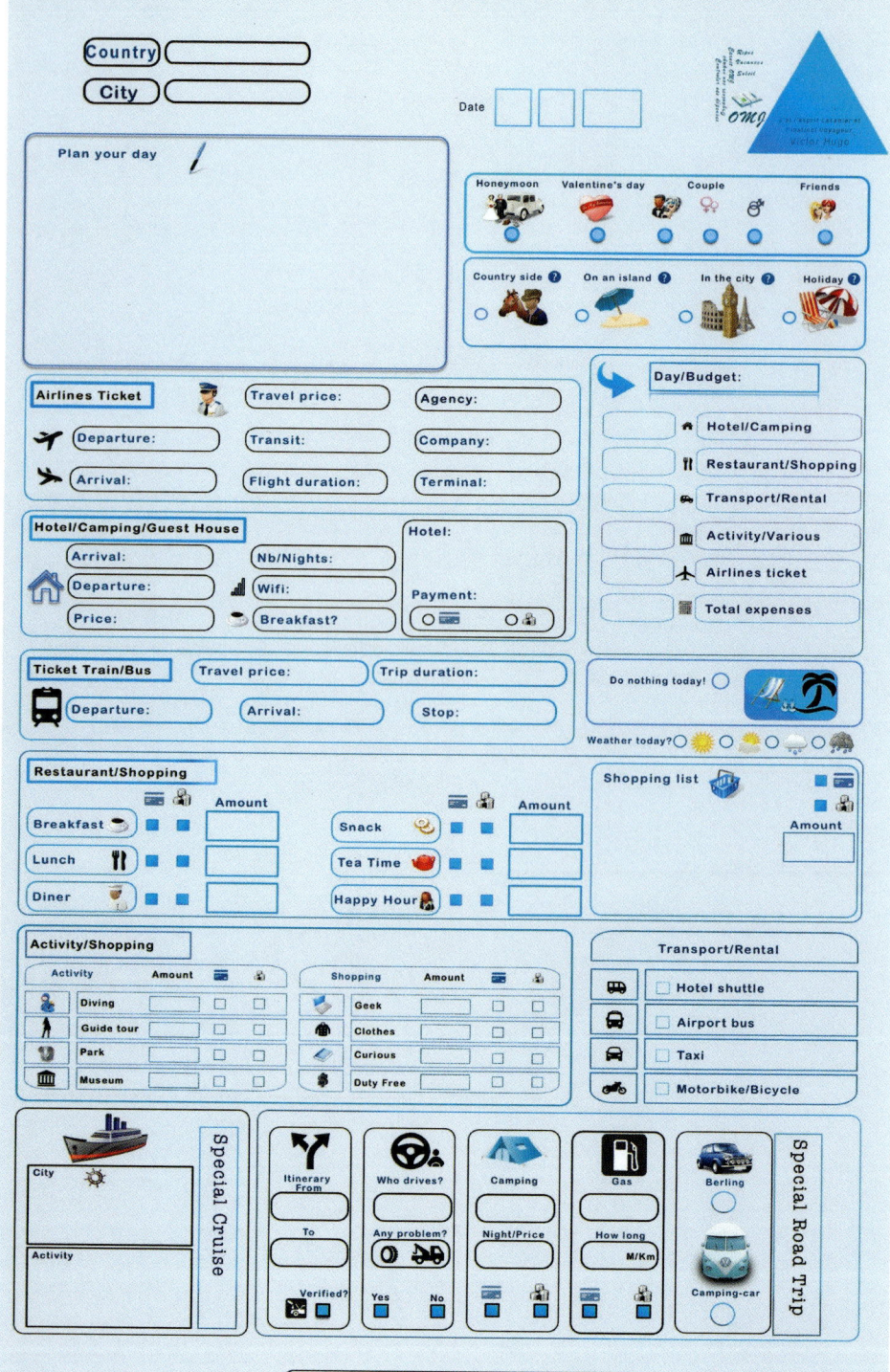

City

Date

Plan your day

Honeymoon   Valentine's day   Couple   Friends

Country side ?   On an island ?   In the city ?   Holiday ?

Day/Budget:

- Hotel/Camping
- Restaurant/Shopping
- Transport/Rental
- Activity/Various
- Airlines ticket
- Total expenses

Airlines Ticket
- Travel price:
- Agency:
- Departure:
- Transit:
- Company:
- Arrival:
- Flight duration:
- Terminal:

Hotel/Camping/Guest House
- Arrival:
- Nb/Nights:
- Hotel:
- Departure:
- Wifi:
- Price:
- Breakfast?
- Payment:

Ticket Train/Bus
- Travel price:
- Trip duration:
- Departure:
- Arrival:
- Stop:

Do nothing today!

Weather today?

Restaurant/Shopping
	Amount		Amount
Breakfast		Snack	
Lunch		Tea Time	
Diner		Happy Hour	

Shopping list
Amount

Activity/Shopping

Activity	Amount		Shopping	Amount	
Diving			Geek		
Guide tour			Clothes		
Park			Curious		
Museum			Duty Free		

Transport/Rental
- Hotel shuttle
- Airport bus
- Taxi
- Motorbike/Bicycle

Special Cruise
City
Activity

Itinerary From
To
Verified?

Who drives?
Any problem?
Yes   No

Camping
Night/Price

Gas
How long
M/Km

Special Road Trip
Berling
Camping-car

How to prepare a trip.
www.vahine-production.com

Note

Bali
Chili
Philippines
Île de Pâques
Mexique
Perou
Bresil
Argentine
USA
Nouvelle-Zelande
Angleterre
Californie
Polynésie Française
Portugal
Singapour
France
Corée
Cambodge
Malaisie
Nepal
Laos
Tibet
Espagne
La Reunion
Hawaii
Les Antilles
Norvège
Thailande
Grèce
Chine
Inde
Seychelles
Madagascar
Belgique
Islande
Vietnam
Italie
Australie
Japon
Danemark
Allemagne
Roumanie
Guyane
Taiwan
Russie
Estonie
Suisse

Country

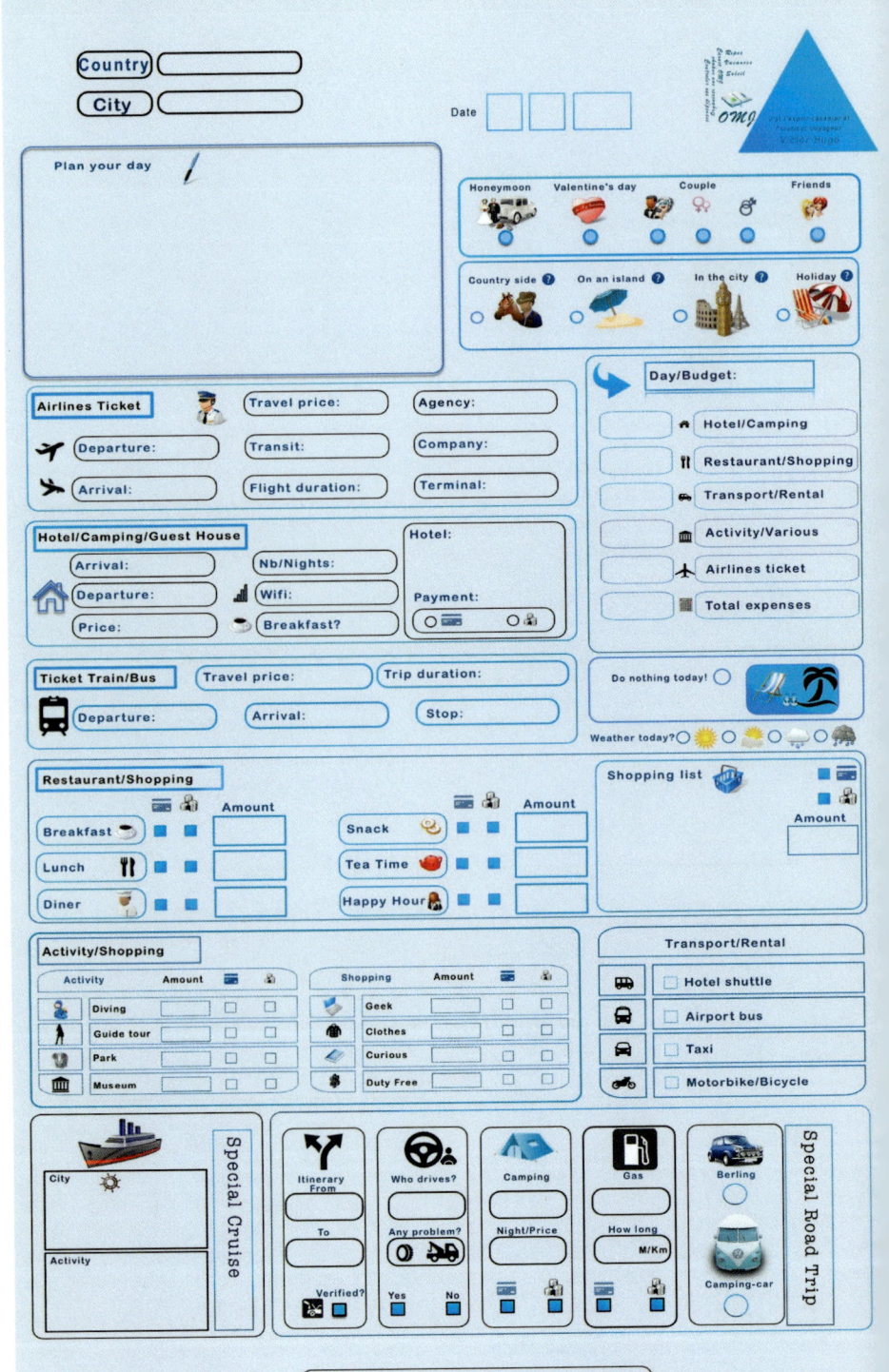

City

Date

Plan your day

Honeymoon Valentine's day Couple Friends

Country side ? On an island ? In the city ? Holiday ?

Airlines Ticket
- Travel price:
- Agency:
- Departure:
- Transit:
- Company:
- Arrival:
- Flight duration:
- Terminal:

Hotel/Camping/Guest House
- Hotel:
- Arrival:
- Nb/Nights:
- Departure:
- Wifi:
- Payment:
- Price:
- Breakfast?

Ticket Train/Bus
- Travel price:
- Trip duration:
- Departure:
- Arrival:
- Stop:

Day/Budget:
- Hotel/Camping
- Restaurant/Shopping
- Transport/Rental
- Activity/Various
- Airlines ticket
- Total expenses

Do nothing today!

Weather today?

Restaurant/Shopping
- Breakfast — Amount
- Lunch — Amount
- Diner
- Snack
- Tea Time
- Happy Hour

Shopping list
Amount

Activity/Shopping

Activity	Amount
Diving	
Guide tour	
Park	
Museum	

Shopping	Amount
Geek	
Clothes	
Curious	
Duty Free	

Transport/Rental
- Hotel shuttle
- Airport bus
- Taxi
- Motorbike/Bicycle

City / Activity — **Special Cruise**

Itinerary From / To — Who drives? — Any problem? — Verified? Yes No

Camping — Night/Price

Gas — How long M/Km

Berling / Camping-car — **Special Road Trip**

How to prepare a trip.
www.vahine-production.com

Note

Bali
Chili
Philippines
Île de Pâques
Mexique
Pérou
Brésil
Argentine
USA
Nouvelle-Zélande
Angleterre
Californie
Polynésie Française
Portugal
France
Corée
Singapour
$
Cambodge
Malaisie
Népal
£
Laos
¥
Tibet
€
Espagne
La Reunion
Hawaii
Les Antilles
Norvège

Thailande
Grèce
Chine
Inde
Seychelles
Madagascar
Belgique
Islande
Vietnam
Italie
Australie
Japon
Danemark
Allemagne
Guyane
Roumanie
Taïwan
Russie
Estonie
Suisse

French Touch

Travel Planning Sheet

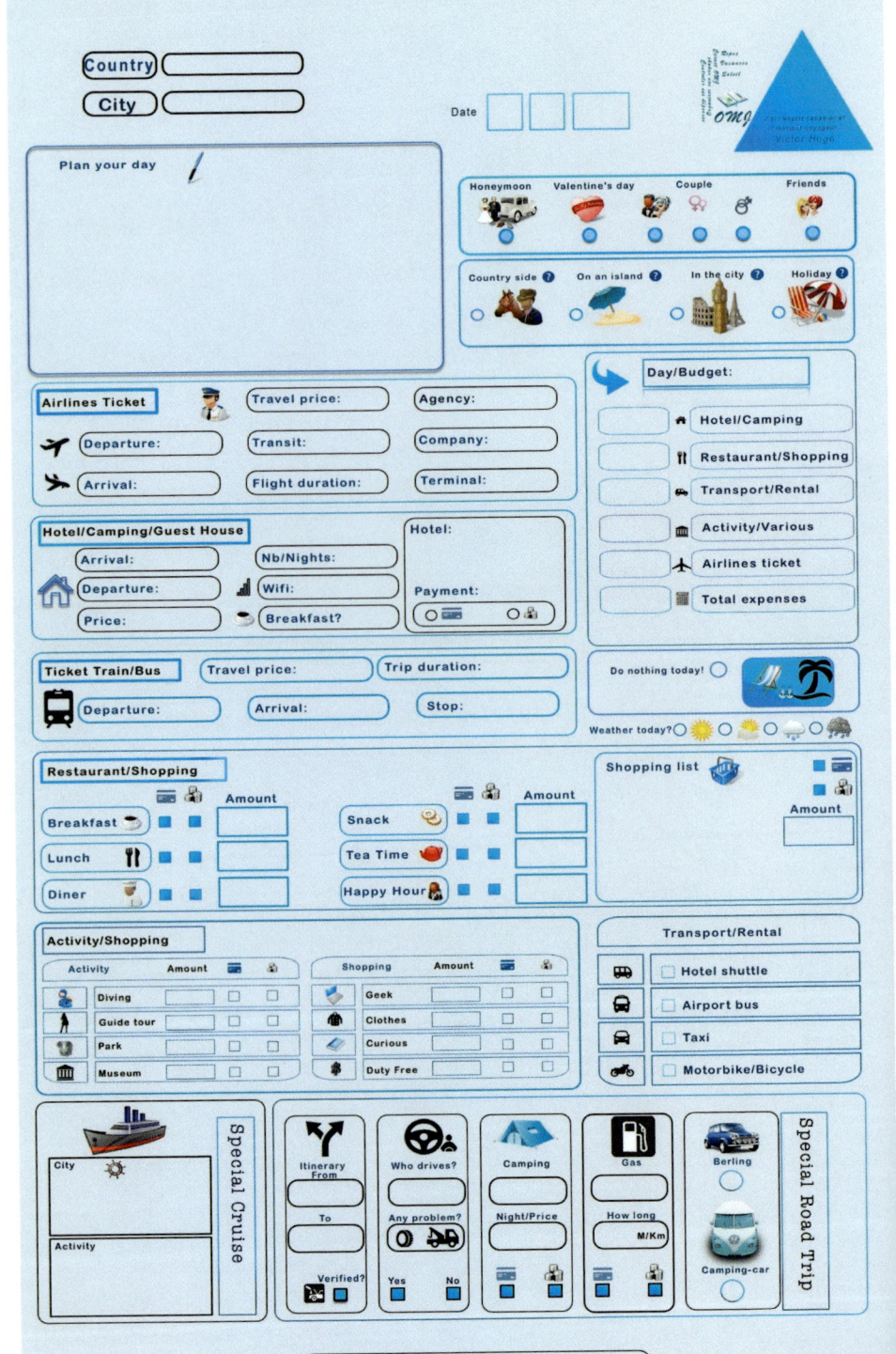

Country: _____
City: _____
Date: __ / __ / __

Plan your day

_____

Trip Type
- Honeymoon
- Valentine's day
- Couple
- Friends

- Country side ?
- On an island ?
- In the city ?
- Holiday ?

Airlines Ticket
- Travel price: _____
- Agency: _____
- Departure: _____
- Transit: _____
- Company: _____
- Arrival: _____
- Flight duration: _____
- Terminal: _____

Hotel/Camping/Guest House
- Arrival: _____
- Nb/Nights: _____
- Hotel: _____
- Departure: _____
- Wifi: _____
- Payment: _____
- Price: _____
- Breakfast? _____

Day/Budget:
- Hotel/Camping
- Restaurant/Shopping
- Transport/Rental
- Activity/Various
- Airlines ticket
- Total expenses

Ticket Train/Bus
- Travel price: _____
- Trip duration: _____
- Departure: _____
- Arrival: _____
- Stop: _____

Do nothing today! ○

Weather today? ○ ○ ○ ○

Restaurant/Shopping
	Amount
Breakfast	
Lunch	
Diner	
Snack	
Tea Time	
Happy Hour	

Shopping list
Amount: _____

Activity/Shopping

Activity — Amount
- Diving
- Guide tour
- Park
- Museum

Shopping — Amount
- Geek
- Clothes
- Curious
- Duty Free

Transport/Rental
- Hotel shuttle
- Airport bus
- Taxi
- Motorbike/Bicycle

Special Cruise
- City
- Activity

Special Road Trip
- Itinerary From / To
- Who drives?
- Camping
- Gas
- Berling
- Any problem?
- Night/Price
- How long M/Km
- Camping-car
- Verified? Yes / No

How to prepare a trip.
www.vahine-production.com

Note

Bali
Chili
Mexique
Pérou
Brésil
Argentine
USA
Nouvelle-Zélande
Angleterre
Californie
Polynésie Française
Portugal
France
Corée
Cambodge
Népal
Laos
Tibet
Singapour
Malaisie
Île de Pâques
Philippines
$
£
¥
€
Espagne
La Réunion
Hawaii
Les Antilles
Norvège
Thaïlande
Grèce
Chine
Inde
Seychelles
Madagascar
Belgique
Islande
Vietnam
Italie
Australie
Japon
Danemark
Allemagne
Roumanie
Guyane
Taiwan
Russie
Estonie
Suisse

French Touch

Country

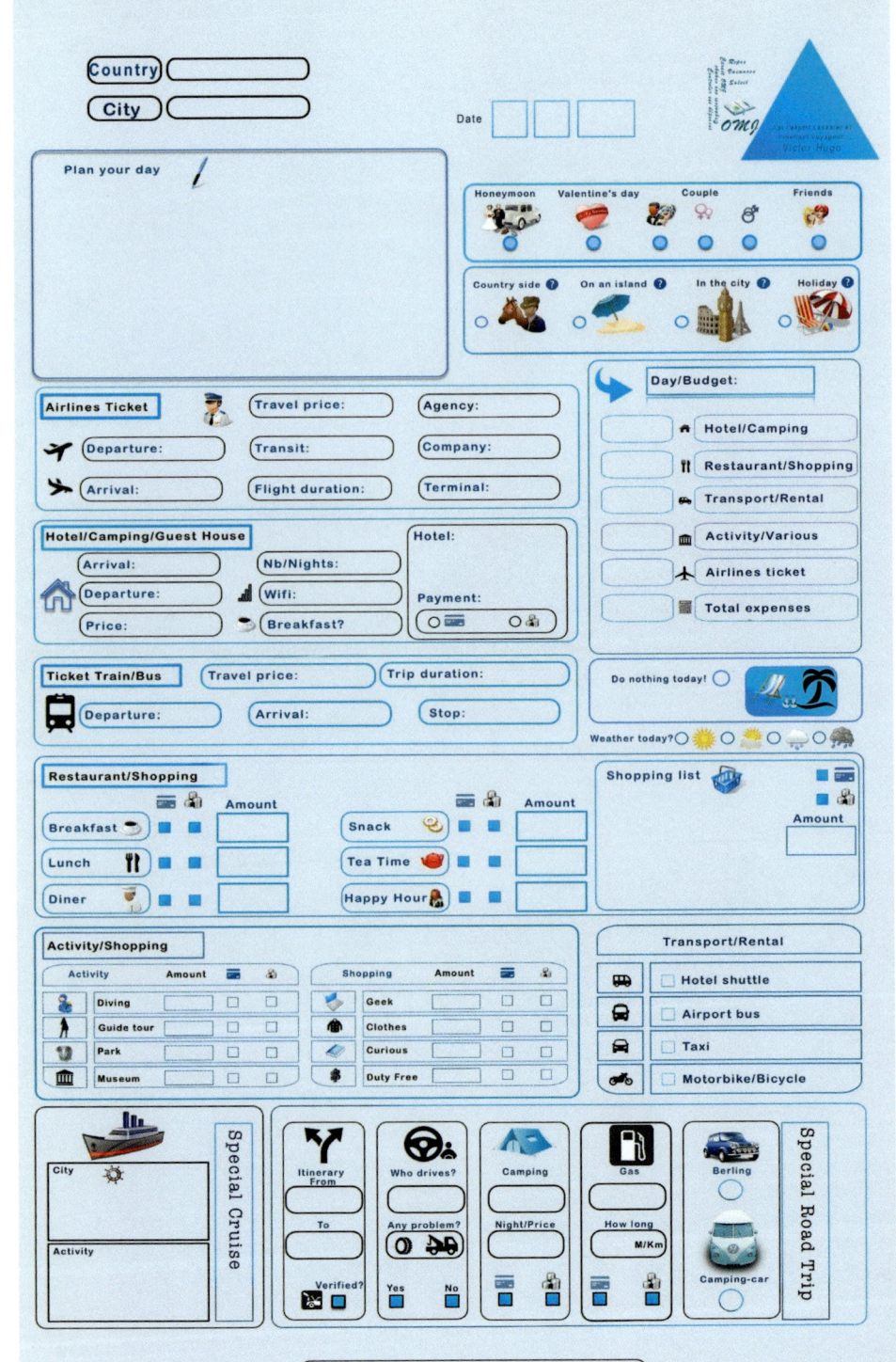

City

Date

Plan your day

Honeymoon Valentine's day Couple Friends

Country side On an island In the city Holiday

Airlines Ticket
- Travel price:
- Agency:
- Departure:
- Transit:
- Company:
- Arrival:
- Flight duration:
- Terminal:

Hotel/Camping/Guest House
- Arrival:
- Nb/Nights:
- Hotel:
- Departure:
- Wifi:
- Price:
- Breakfast?
- Payment:

Ticket Train/Bus
- Travel price:
- Trip duration:
- Departure:
- Arrival:
- Stop:

Day/Budget:
- Hotel/Camping
- Restaurant/Shopping
- Transport/Rental
- Activity/Various
- Airlines ticket
- Total expenses

Do nothing today!

Weather today?

Restaurant/Shopping
- Breakfast — Amount
- Lunch
- Diner
- Snack
- Tea Time
- Happy Hour

Shopping list — Amount

Activity/Shopping

Activity	Amount		
Diving			
Guide tour			
Park			
Museum			

Shopping	Amount		
Geek			
Clothes			
Curious			
Duty Free			

Transport/Rental
- Hotel shuttle
- Airport bus
- Taxi
- Motorbike/Bicycle

Special Cruise
- City
- Activity

- Itinerary From
- To
- Verified?
- Who drives?
- Any problem?
- Yes / No
- Camping
- Night/Price
- Gas
- How long M/Km

Special Road Trip
- Berling
- Camping-car

How to prepare a trip.
www.vahine-production.com

Note

Bali
Chili
Mexique
Philippines
Pérou
Brésil
Île de Pâques
Argentine
USA
Sénégal
Nouvelle-Zélande
Angleterre
Californie
Polynésie Française
Portugal
France
Singapour
Corée
Cambodge
$
Nepal
£
Malaisie
Laos
¥
Tibet
€
Espagne
La Reunion
Hawaii
Les Antilles
Norvège
Thailande
Grèce
Chine
Inde
Seychelles
Madagascar
Belgique
Islande
Vietnam
Italie
Australie
Japon
Danemark
Allemagne
Guyane
Roumanie
Taiwan
Russie
Estonie
Suisse

French Touch

Country
City
Date

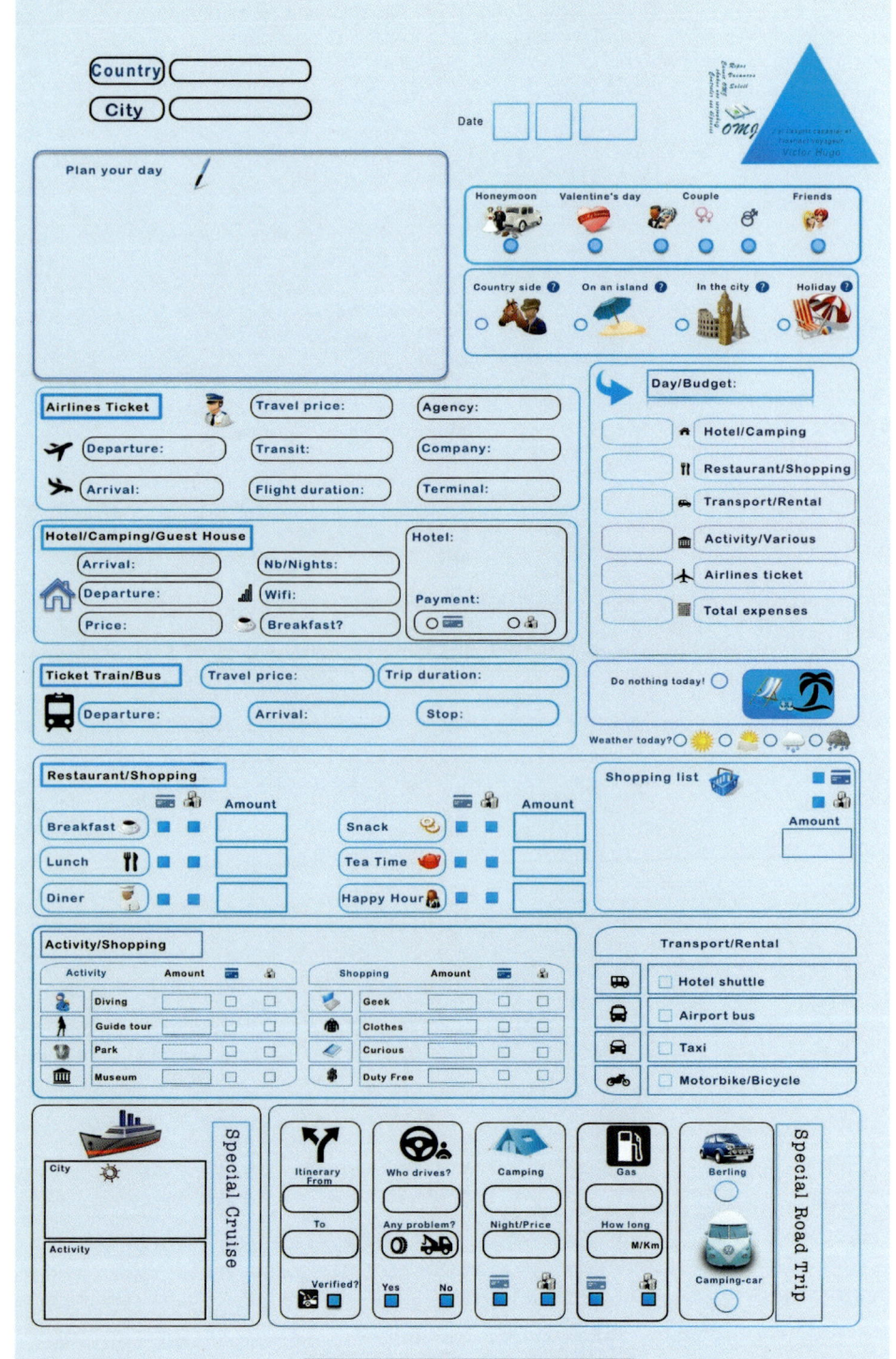

Plan your day

Honeymoon Valentine's day Couple Friends

Country side On an island In the city Holiday

Airlines Ticket
- Travel price:
- Agency:
- Departure:
- Transit:
- Company:
- Arrival:
- Flight duration:
- Terminal:

Hotel/Camping/Guest House
- Arrival:
- Nb/Nights:
- Hotel:
- Departure:
- Wifi:
- Payment:
- Price:
- Breakfast?

Day/Budget:
- Hotel/Camping
- Restaurant/Shopping
- Transport/Rental
- Activity/Various
- Airlines ticket
- Total expenses

Ticket Train/Bus
- Travel price:
- Trip duration:
- Departure:
- Arrival:
- Stop:

Do nothing today!

Weather today?

Restaurant/Shopping
	Amount		Amount
Breakfast		Snack	
Lunch		Tea Time	
Diner		Happy Hour	

Shopping list
Amount

Activity/Shopping
Activity	Amount		Shopping	Amount	
Diving			Geek		
Guide tour			Clothes		
Park			Curious		
Museum			Duty Free		

Transport/Rental
- Hotel shuttle
- Airport bus
- Taxi
- Motorbike/Bicycle

Special Cruise
City
Activity

Special Road Trip
- Itinerary From / To
- Who drives? / Any problem?
- Camping / Night/Price
- Gas / How long M/Km
- Berling / Camping-car
- Verified? Yes No

How to prepare a trip.
www.vahine-production.com

Note

Bali
Chili
Philippines
Mexique
Île de Pâques
Pérou
Brésil
Argentine
USA
Nouvelle-Zélande
Angleterre
Californie
Polynésie Française
Portugal
Singapour
France
Corée
$
Cambodge
Malaisie
£
Népal
¥
Laos
Tibet
€
Espagne
La Réunion
Hawaii
Les Antilles
Norvège

Thaïlande
Grèce   Chine
Inde
Seychelles
Madagascar
Belgique
Islande
Vietnam
Italie
Australie
Japon
Danemark
Allemagne   Guyane
Roumanie   Taiwan
Russie
Estonie
Suisse

French Touch

Country

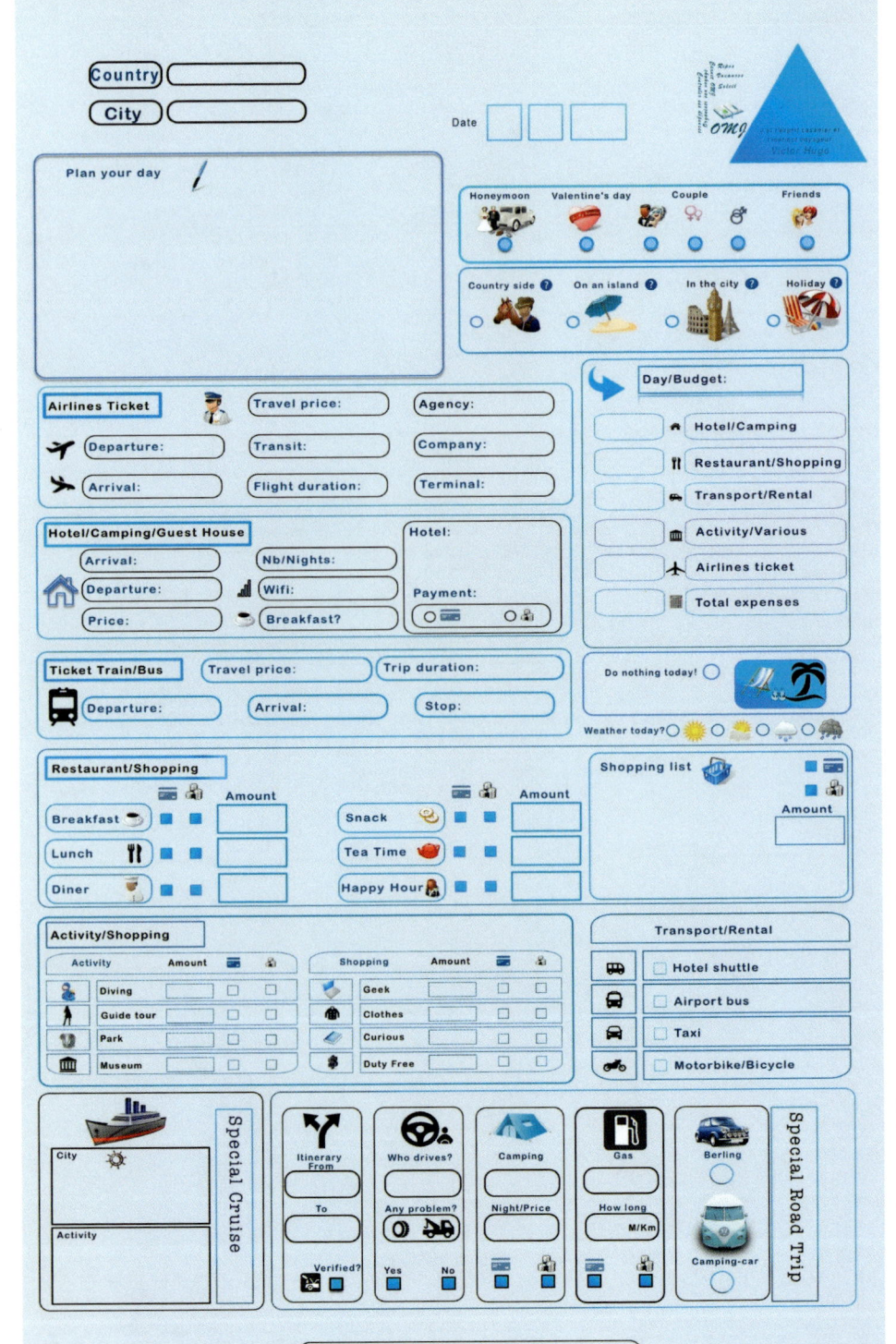

City

Date

Plan your day

Honeymoon Valentine's day Couple Friends

Country side On an island In the city Holiday

Airlines Ticket
- Travel price:
- Agency:
- Departure:
- Transit:
- Company:
- Arrival:
- Flight duration:
- Terminal:

Day/Budget:
- Hotel/Camping
- Restaurant/Shopping
- Transport/Rental
- Activity/Various
- Airlines ticket
- Total expenses

Hotel/Camping/Guest House
- Arrival:
- Nb/Nights:
- Hotel:
- Departure:
- Wifi:
- Payment:
- Price:
- Breakfast?

Ticket Train/Bus
- Travel price:
- Trip duration:
- Departure:
- Arrival:
- Stop:

Do nothing today!

Weather today?

Restaurant/Shopping
- Breakfast — Amount
- Lunch
- Diner
- Snack
- Tea Time
- Happy Hour

Shopping list — Amount

Activity/Shopping

Activity	Amount		
Diving			
Guide tour			
Park			
Museum			

Shopping	Amount		
Geek			
Clothes			
Curious			
Duty Free			

Transport/Rental
- Hotel shuttle
- Airport bus
- Taxi
- Motorbike/Bicycle

Special Cruise
- City
- Activity

- Itinerary From
- To
- Verified?

- Who drives?
- Any problem?
- Yes / No

- Camping
- Night/Price

- Gas
- How long
- M/Km

Special Road Trip
- Berling
- Camping-car

How to prepare a trip.
www.vahine-production.com

Note

Bali
Chili
Philippines
Île de Pâques
Mexique
Perou
Bresil
Argentine
USA
Nouvelle-Zelande
Angleterre
Californie
Polynésie Française
Portugal
France
Corée
Singapour
Cambodge
Malaisie
Nepal
Laos
Tibet
Espagne
La Reunion
Hawaii
Les Antilles
Norvège
Thailande
Grèce
Chine
Inde
Seychelles
Madagascar
Belgique
Islande
Vietnam
Italie
Australie
Japon
Danemark
Allemagne
Guyane
Taiwan
Roumanie
Russie
Estonie
Suisse

French Touch

Country

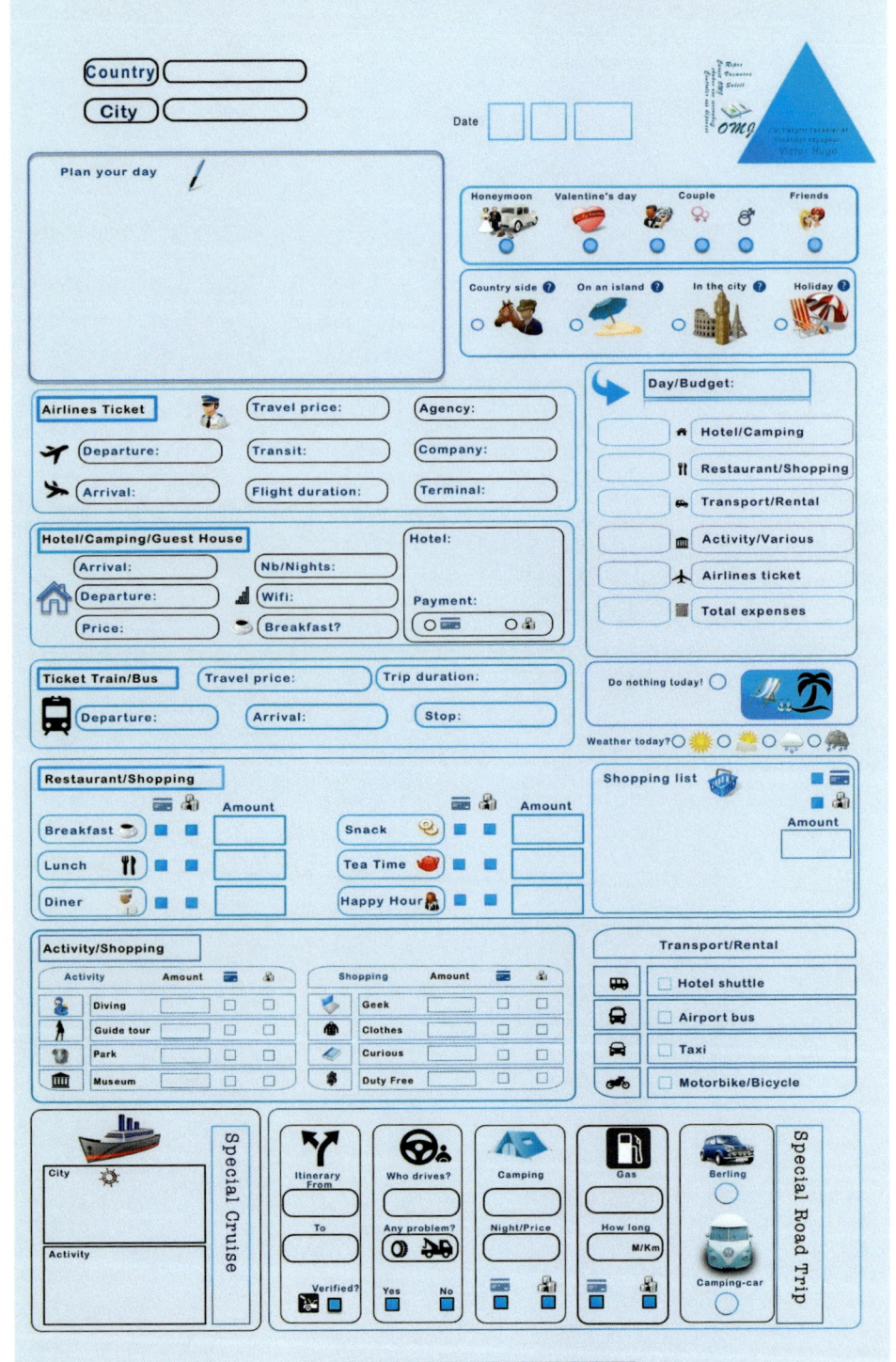

City

Date

Plan your day

Honeymoon | Valentine's day | Couple | Friends

Country side | On an island | In the city | Holiday

Airlines Ticket
- Travel price:
- Agency:
- Departure:
- Transit:
- Company:
- Arrival:
- Flight duration:
- Terminal:

Hotel/Camping/Guest House
- Arrival:
- Nb/Nights:
- Hotel:
- Departure:
- Wifi:
- Payment:
- Price:
- Breakfast?

Ticket Train/Bus
- Travel price:
- Trip duration:
- Departure:
- Arrival:
- Stop:

Day/Budget:
- Hotel/Camping
- Restaurant/Shopping
- Transport/Rental
- Activity/Various
- Airlines ticket
- Total expenses

Do nothing today!

Weather today?

Restaurant/Shopping
- Breakfast — Amount
- Lunch
- Diner
- Snack
- Tea Time
- Happy Hour

Shopping list — Amount

Activity/Shopping

Activity | Amount
- Diving
- Guide tour
- Park
- Museum

Shopping | Amount
- Geek
- Clothes
- Curious
- Duty Free

Transport/Rental
- Hotel shuttle
- Airport bus
- Taxi
- Motorbike/Bicycle

Special Cruise
- City
- Activity

- Itinerary From
- To
- Verified?

- Who drives?
- Any problem?
- Yes / No

- Camping
- Night/Price

- Gas
- How long M/Km

Special Road Trip
- Berling
- Camping-car

How to prepare a trip.
www.vahine-production.com

Note

Bali
Chili
Philippines
Île de Pâques
Mexique
Pérou
Brésil
Argentine
USA
Nouvelle-Zélande
Angleterre
Californie
Polynésie Française
Portugal
France
Corée
Cambodge
Singapour
Malaisie
Népal
Laos
Tibet
Espagne
La Réunion
Hawaii
Les Antilles
Norvège
Thaïlande
Grèce
Chine
Inde
Seychelles
Madagascar
Belgique
Islande
Vietnam
Italie
Australie
Japon
Danemark
Allemagne
Roumanie
Guyane
Taïwan
Russie
Estonie
Suisse

French Touch

Country
City
Date

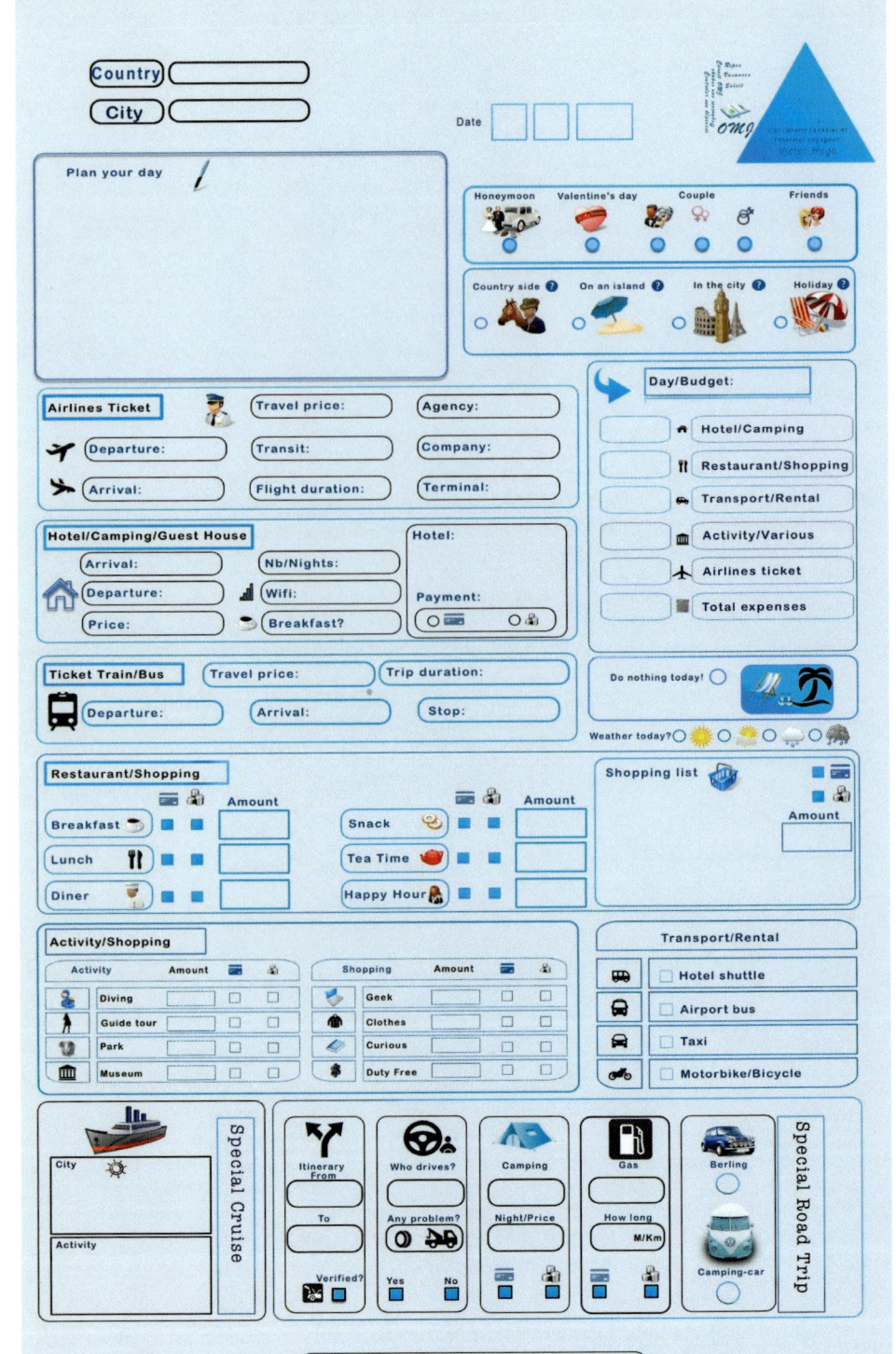

Plan your day

Honeymoon Valentine's day Couple Friends

Country side On an island In the city Holiday

Airlines Ticket
- Travel price:
- Departure:
- Transit:
- Agency:
- Company:
- Arrival:
- Flight duration:
- Terminal:

Hotel/Camping/Guest House
- Arrival:
- Nb/Nights:
- Hotel:
- Departure:
- Wifi:
- Price:
- Breakfast?
- Payment:

Day/Budget:
- Hotel/Camping
- Restaurant/Shopping
- Transport/Rental
- Activity/Various
- Airlines ticket
- Total expenses

Ticket Train/Bus
- Travel price:
- Trip duration:
- Departure:
- Arrival:
- Stop:

Do nothing today!

Weather today?

Restaurant/Shopping
- Breakfast — Amount
- Lunch
- Diner
- Snack — Amount
- Tea Time
- Happy Hour

Shopping list — Amount

Activity/Shopping

Activity	Amount			Shopping	Amount		
Diving				Geek			
Guide tour				Clothes			
Park				Curious			
Museum				Duty Free			

Transport/Rental
- Hotel shuttle
- Airport bus
- Taxi
- Motorbike/Bicycle

City
Activity

Special Cruise

Itinerary From
To
Verified?

Who drives?
Any problem?
Yes No

Camping
Night/Price

Gas
How long M/Km

Berling
Camping-car

Special Road Trip

How to prepare a trip.
www.vahine-production.com

Note

Bali
Chili
Philippines
Île de Pâques
Mexique
Perou
Bresil
Argentine
USA
Nouvelle-Zelande
Angleterre
Californie
Polynésie Française
Portugal
France
Corée
Cambodge
Singapour
Malaisie
$
£
¥
€
Nepal
Laos
Tibet
Espagne
La Reunion
Hawaii
Les Antilles
Norvège
Thailande
Grèce
Chine
Inde
Seychelles
Madagascar
Belgique
Islande
Vietnam
Italie
Australie
Japon
Danemark
Allemagne
Roumanie
Guyane
Taiwan
Russie
Estonie
Suisse

French Touch

Country
City
Date

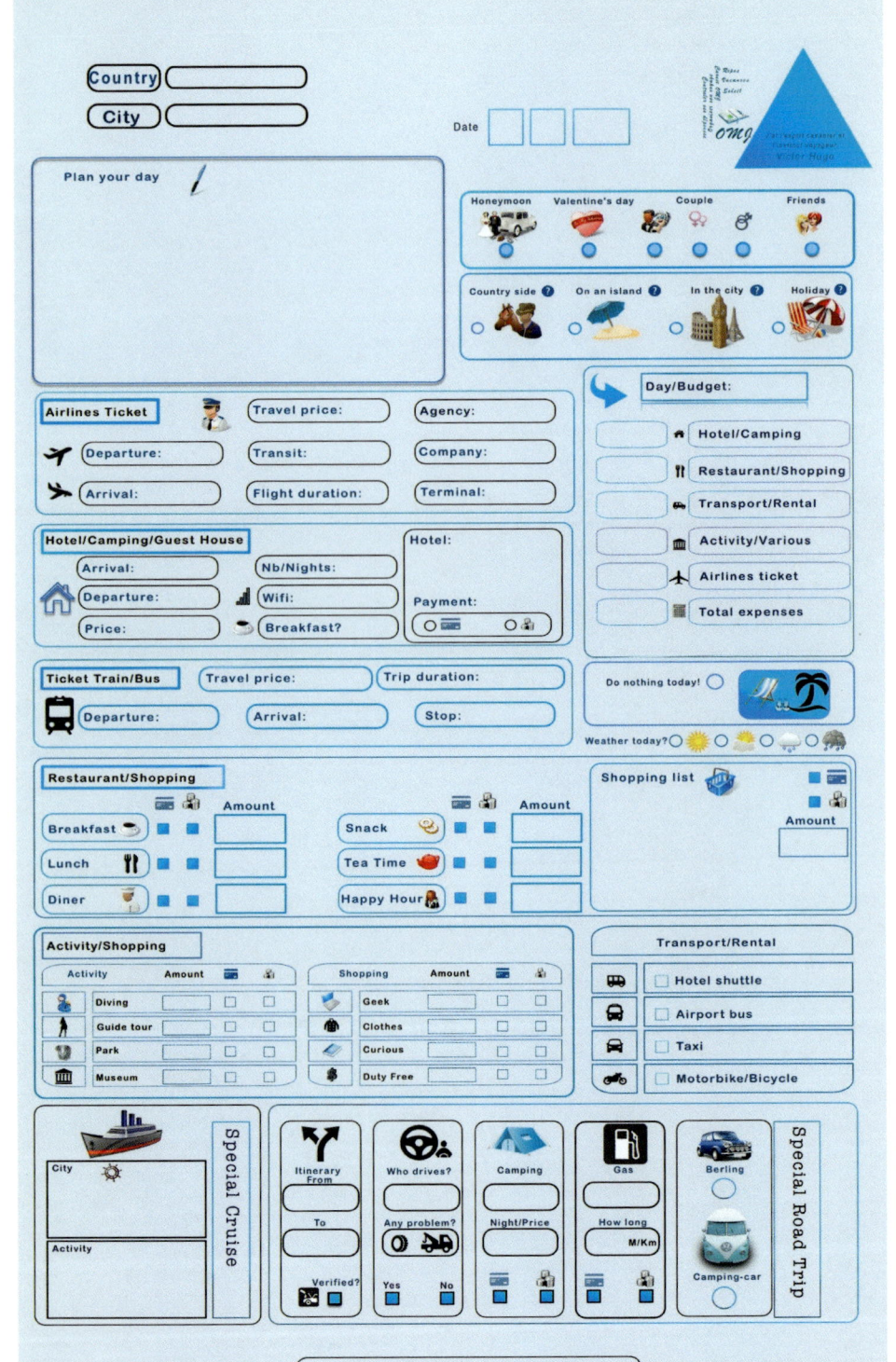

Plan your day

Honeymoon | Valentine's day | Couple | Friends

Country side | On an island | In the city | Holiday

Airlines Ticket
- Travel price:
- Agency:
- Departure:
- Transit:
- Company:
- Arrival:
- Flight duration:
- Terminal:

Hotel/Camping/Guest House
- Arrival:
- Nb/Nights:
- Hotel:
- Departure:
- Wifi:
- Payment:
- Price:
- Breakfast?

Ticket Train/Bus
- Travel price:
- Trip duration:
- Departure:
- Arrival:
- Stop:

Day/Budget:
- Hotel/Camping
- Restaurant/Shopping
- Transport/Rental
- Activity/Various
- Airlines ticket
- Total expenses

Do nothing today!

Weather today?

Restaurant/Shopping
- Breakfast — Amount
- Snack — Amount
- Lunch
- Tea Time
- Diner
- Happy Hour

Shopping list
- Amount

Activity/Shopping

Activity | Amount
- Diving
- Guide tour
- Park
- Museum

Shopping | Amount
- Geek
- Clothes
- Curious
- Duty Free

Transport/Rental
- Hotel shuttle
- Airport bus
- Taxi
- Motorbike/Bicycle

Special Cruise
- City
- Activity

- Itinerary From
- To
- Verified?

- Who drives?
- Any problem?
- Yes / No

- Camping
- Night/Price

- Gas
- How long M/Km

Special Road Trip
- Berling
- Camping-car

How to prepare a trip.
www.vahine-production.com

Note

Bali
Chili
Philippines
Mexique
Pérou
Brésil
Argentine
USA
Nouvelle-Zélande
Angleterre
Californie
Polynésie Française
Portugal
France
Corée
Cambodge
Singapour
Malaisie
Népal
Laos
Tibet
Espagne
La Réunion
Hawaii
Les Antilles
Norvège
Thaïlande
Grèce Chine
Inde
Seychelles
Madagascar
Belgique
Islande
Vietnam
Italie
Australie
Japon
Danemark
Allemagne
Roumanie
Guyane
Taïwan
Russie
Estonie
Suisse

French Touch

Country

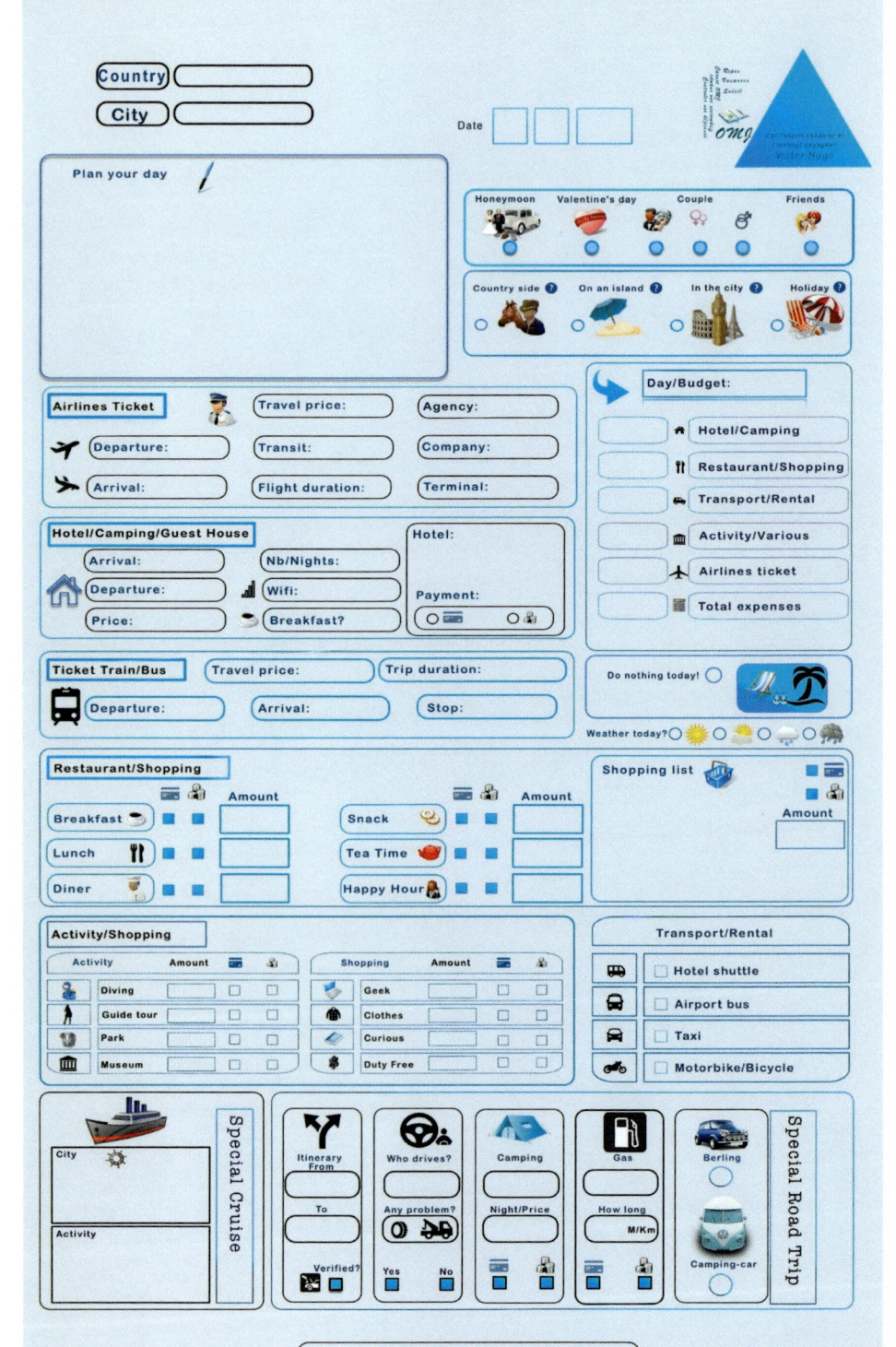

City

Date

Plan your day

Honeymoon   Valentine's day   Couple   Friends

Country side   On an island   In the city   Holiday

Airlines Ticket
- Travel price:
- Agency:
- Departure:
- Transit:
- Company:
- Arrival:
- Flight duration:
- Terminal:

Day/Budget:
- Hotel/Camping
- Restaurant/Shopping
- Transport/Rental
- Activity/Various
- Airlines ticket
- Total expenses

Hotel/Camping/Guest House
- Arrival:
- Nb/Nights:
- Hotel:
- Departure:
- Wifi:
- Payment:
- Price:
- Breakfast?

Ticket Train/Bus
- Travel price:
- Trip duration:
- Departure:
- Arrival:
- Stop:

Do nothing today!

Weather today?

Restaurant/Shopping
- Breakfast — Amount
- Lunch — Amount
- Diner
- Snack
- Tea Time
- Happy Hour

Shopping list — Amount

Activity/Shopping

Activity	Amount		Shopping	Amount	
Diving			Geek		
Guide tour			Clothes		
Park			Curious		
Museum			Duty Free		

Transport/Rental
- Hotel shuttle
- Airport bus
- Taxi
- Motorbike/Bicycle

Special Cruise
- City
- Activity

- Itinerary From
- To
- Verified?
- Who drives?
- Any problem?
- Yes / No
- Camping
- Night/Price
- Gas
- How long M/Km

Special Road Trip
- Berling
- Camping-car

How to prepare a trip.
www.vahine-production.com

Note

Bali
Chili
Mexique
Philippines
Île de Pâques
Pérou
Brésil
Argentine
USA
Nouvelle-Zélande
Angleterre
Californie
Polynésie Française
Portugal
France
Corée
Cambodge
Singapour
Malaisie
Népal
Laos
Tibet
Espagne
La Réunion
Hawaii
Les Antilles
Norvège
Thaïlande
Grèce
Chine
Inde
Seychelles
Madagascar
Belgique
Islande
Vietnam
Italie
Australie
Japon
Danemark
Allemagne
Roumanie
Guyane
Taiwan
Russie
Estonie
Suisse

French Touch

Country
City
Date

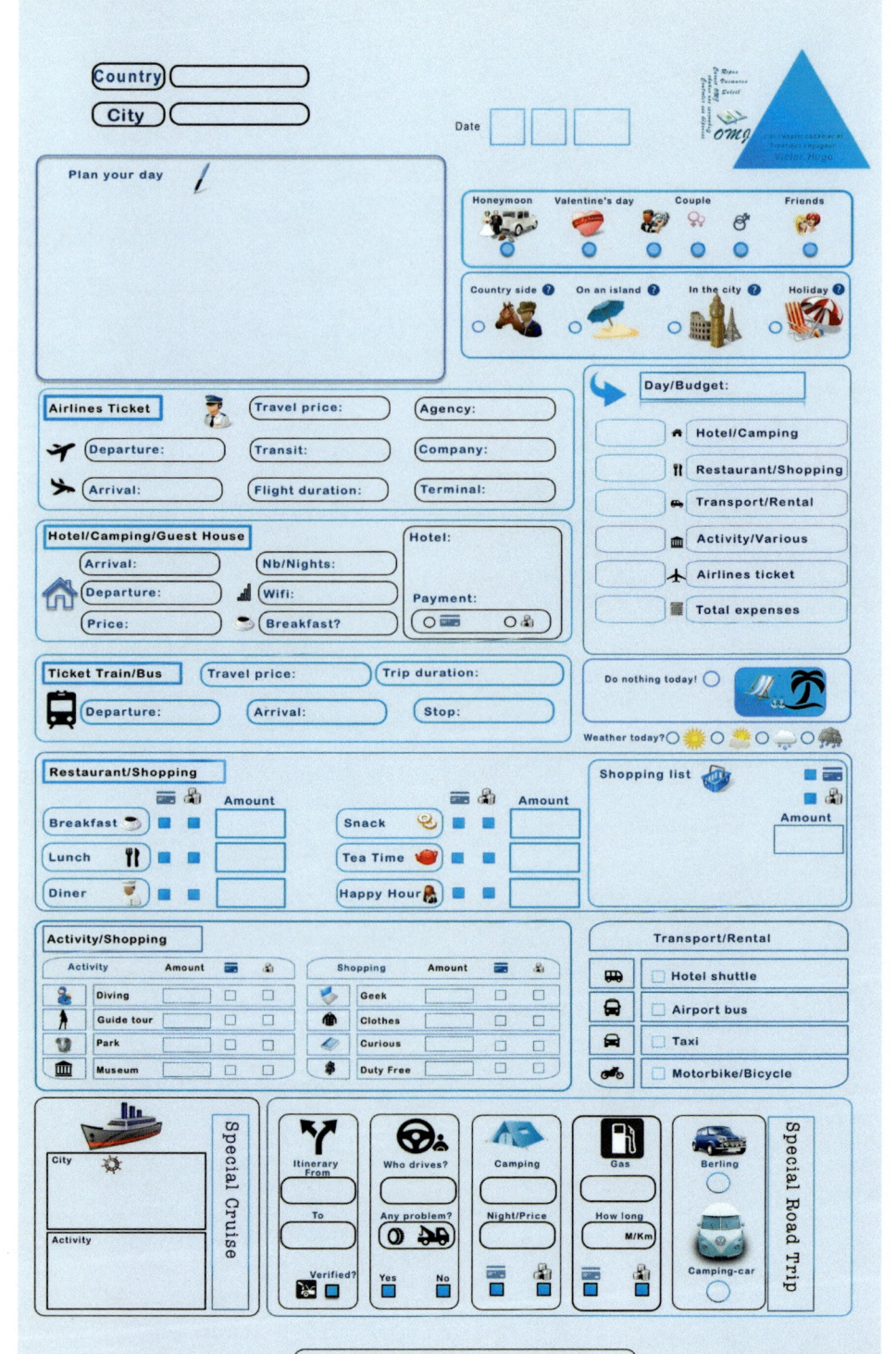

Plan your day

Honeymoon   Valentine's day   Couple   Friends

Country side   On an island   In the city   Holiday

Airlines Ticket
Travel price: Agency:
Departure: Transit: Company:
Arrival: Flight duration: Terminal:

Hotel/Camping/Guest House
Arrival: Nb/Nights: Hotel:
Departure: Wifi: Payment:
Price: Breakfast?

Ticket Train/Bus
Travel price: Trip duration:
Departure: Arrival: Stop:

Day/Budget:
- Hotel/Camping
- Restaurant/Shopping
- Transport/Rental
- Activity/Various
- Airlines ticket
- Total expenses

Do nothing today!

Weather today?

Restaurant/Shopping
| | Amount | | | Amount |
Breakfast   Snack
Lunch   Tea Time
Diner   Happy Hour

Shopping list
Amount

Activity/Shopping
Activity   Amount
- Diving
- Guide tour
- Park
- Museum

Shopping   Amount
- Geek
- Clothes
- Curious
- Duty Free

Transport/Rental
- Hotel shuttle
- Airport bus
- Taxi
- Motorbike/Bicycle

City
Activity

Special Cruise

Itinerary From
To
Verified?

Who drives?
Any problem?
Yes   No

Camping
Night/Price

Gas
How long
M/Km

Berlingo
Camping-car

Special Road Trip

How to prepare a trip.
www.vahine-production.com

Note

Bali
Chili
Philippines
Île de Pâques
Mexique
Perou
Bresil
Argentine
USA
Nouvelle-Zelande
Angleterre
Californie
Polynésie Française
Portugal
Singapour
France
Corée
Cambodge
$
€
£
¥
Malaisie
Nepal
Laos
Tibet
€
Espagne
La Reunion
Hawaii
Les Antilles
Norvège
Thailande
Grèce
Chine
Inde
Seychelles
Madagascar
Belgique
Islande
Vietnam
Italie
Australie
Japon
Danemark
Allemagne
Roumanie
Guyane
Taiwan
Russie
Estonie
Suisse

French Touch

Country
City
Date

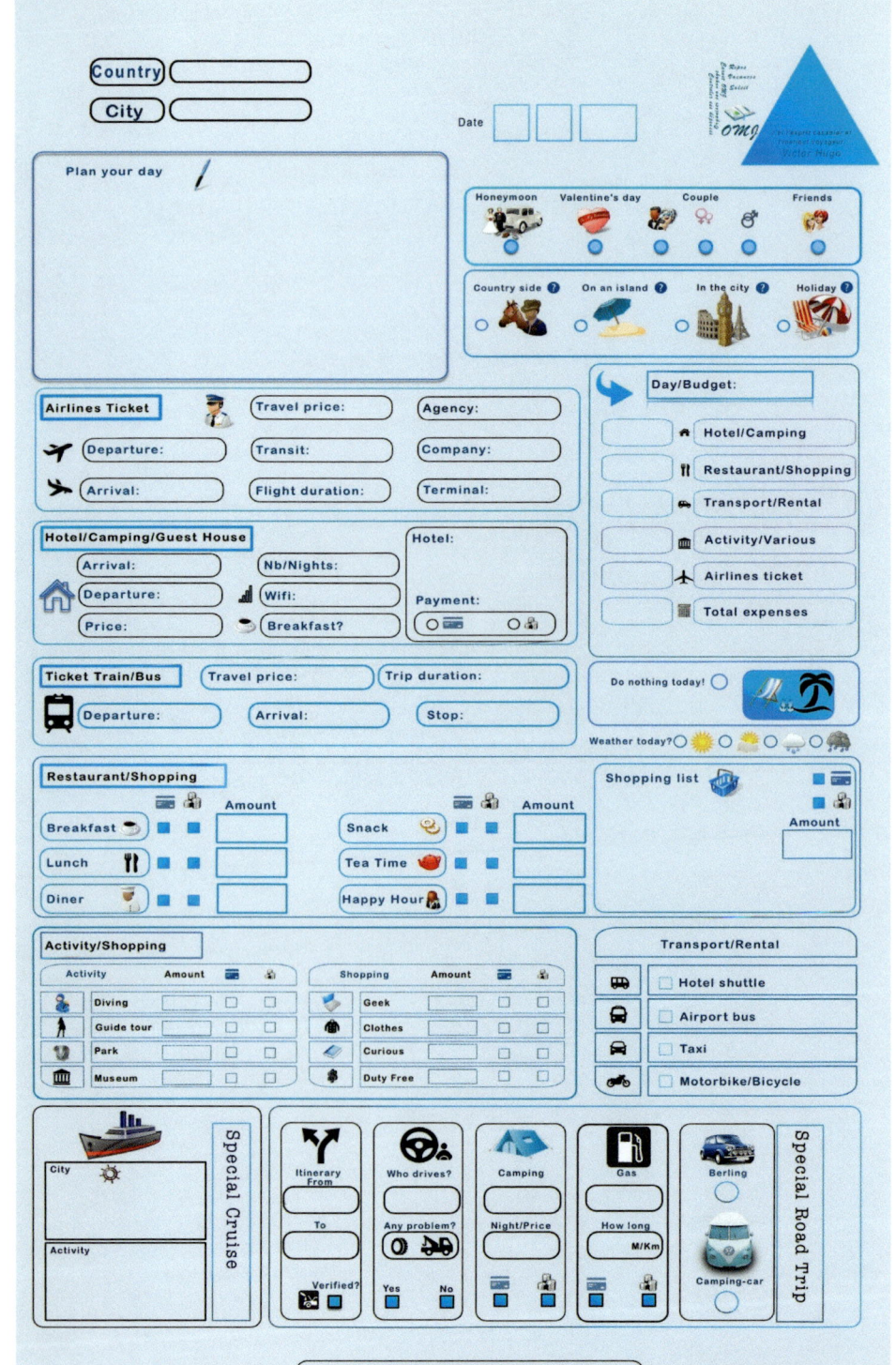

Plan your day

Honeymoon · Valentine's day · Couple · Friends

Country side · On an island · In the city · Holiday

Airlines Ticket
- Travel price:
- Agency:
- Departure:
- Transit:
- Company:
- Arrival:
- Flight duration:
- Terminal:

Hotel/Camping/Guest House
- Arrival:
- Nb/Nights:
- Hotel:
- Departure:
- Wifi:
- Payment:
- Price:
- Breakfast?

Ticket Train/Bus
- Travel price:
- Trip duration:
- Departure:
- Arrival:
- Stop:

Day/Budget:
- Hotel/Camping
- Restaurant/Shopping
- Transport/Rental
- Activity/Various
- Airlines ticket
- Total expenses

Do nothing today!

Weather today?

Restaurant/Shopping
	Amount		Amount
Breakfast		Snack	
Lunch		Tea Time	
Diner		Happy Hour	

Shopping list
Amount

Activity/Shopping
Activity	Amount		Shopping	Amount	
Diving			Geek		
Guide tour			Clothes		
Park			Curious		
Museum			Duty Free		

Transport/Rental
- Hotel shuttle
- Airport bus
- Taxi
- Motorbike/Bicycle

Special Cruise
- City
- Activity

- Itinerary From
- To
- Verified?
- Who drives?
- Any problem?
- Yes / No
- Camping
- Night/Price
- Gas
- How long M/Km
- Berling
- Camping-car

Special Road Trip

How to prepare a trip.
www.vahine-production.com

Note

Bali
Chili
Mexique
Pérou
Brésil
Argentine
USA
Nouvelle-Zélande
Angleterre
Californie
Polynésie Française
Portugal
France
Corée
Cambodge
Népal
Laos
Tibet
Singapour
Malaisie
Îles de Pâques
Philippines
$
£
¥
€
Espagne
La Réunion
Hawaii
Les Antilles
Norvège
Thailande
Grèce
Chine
Inde
Seychelles
Madagascar
Belgique
Islande
Vietnam
Italie
Australie
Japon
Danemark
Allemagne
Roumanie
Guyane
Taiwan
Russie
Estonie
Suisse

French Touch

Travel Planner

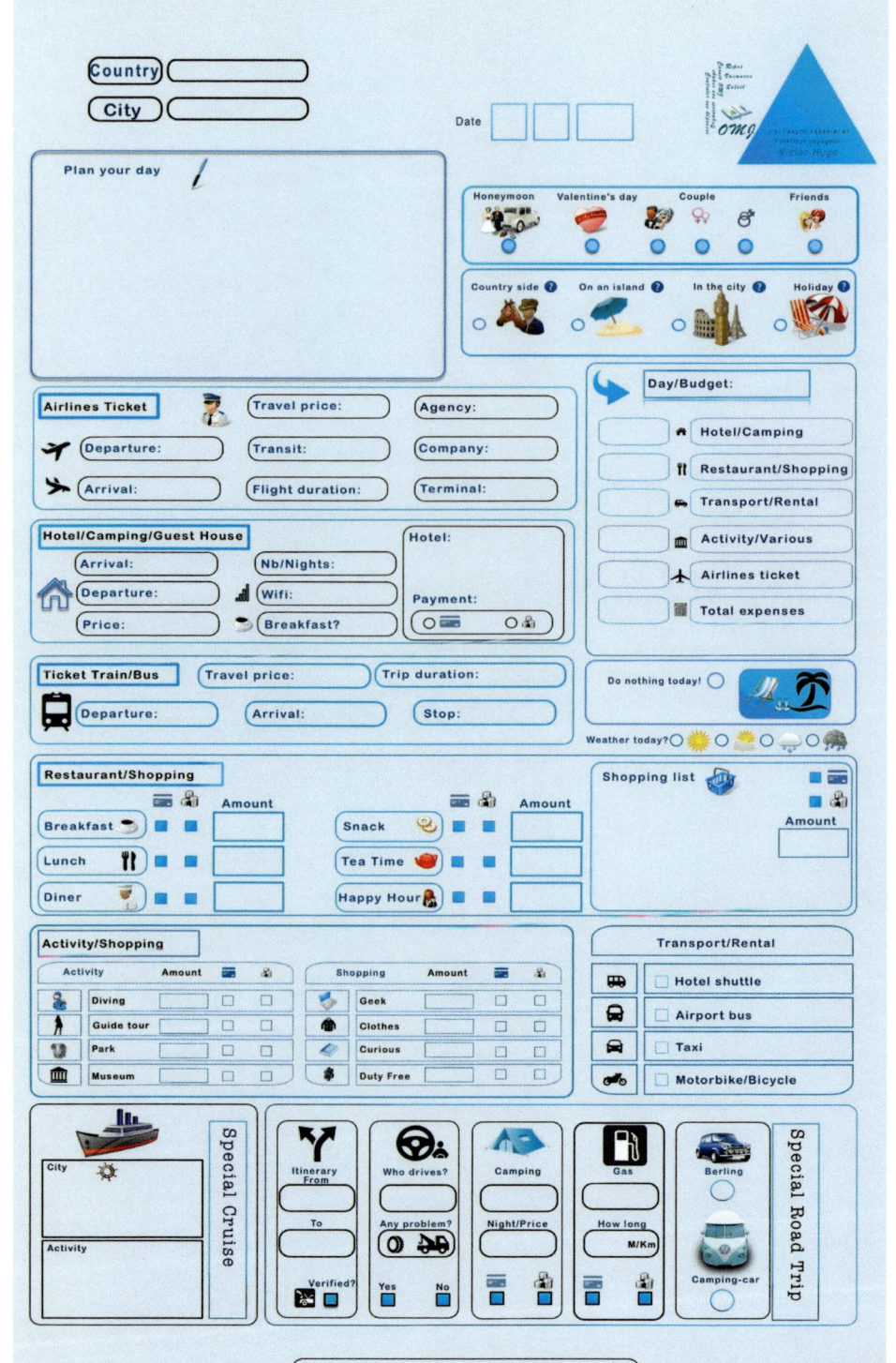

Country: _____
City: _____
Date: ___ ___ ___

Plan your day

- Honeymoon
- Valentine's day
- Couple
- Friends

- Country side
- On an island
- In the city
- Holiday

Airlines Ticket
- Travel price:
- Agency:
- Departure:
- Transit:
- Company:
- Arrival:
- Flight duration:
- Terminal:

Hotel/Camping/Guest House
- Arrival:
- Nb/Nights:
- Hotel:
- Departure:
- Wifi:
- Price:
- Breakfast?
- Payment:

Ticket Train/Bus
- Travel price:
- Trip duration:
- Departure:
- Arrival:
- Stop:

Day/Budget:
- Hotel/Camping
- Restaurant/Shopping
- Transport/Rental
- Activity/Various
- Airlines ticket
- Total expenses

Do nothing today!

Weather today?

Restaurant/Shopping
	Amount			Amount
Breakfast		Snack		
Lunch		Tea Time		
Diner		Happy Hour		

Shopping list
Amount

Activity/Shopping

Activity — Amount
- Diving
- Guide tour
- Park
- Museum

Shopping — Amount
- Geek
- Clothes
- Curious
- Duty Free

Transport/Rental
- Hotel shuttle
- Airport bus
- Taxi
- Motorbike/Bicycle

Special Cruise
- City
- Activity

Itinerary
- From
- To
- Verified?
- Who drives?
- Any problem?
- Yes / No
- Camping
- Night/Price
- Gas
- How long M/Km

Special Road Trip
- Berling
- Camping-car

How to prepare a trip.
www.vahine-production.com

Note

Bali
Chili
Philippines
Île de Pâques
Mexique
Pérou
Brésil
Argentine
USA
Nouvelle-Zélande
Angleterre
Californie
Polynésie Française
Portugal
France
Corée
Cambodge
Singapour
Malaisie
Népal
Laos
Tibet
Espagne
La Réunion
Hawaii
Les Antilles
Norvège
Thaïlande
Grèce Chine
Inde
Seychelles
Madagascar
Belgique
Islande
Vietnam
Italie
Australie
Japon
Danemark
Allemagne
Roumanie
Guyane
Taïwan
Russie
Estonie
Suisse

French Touch

Country
City
Date

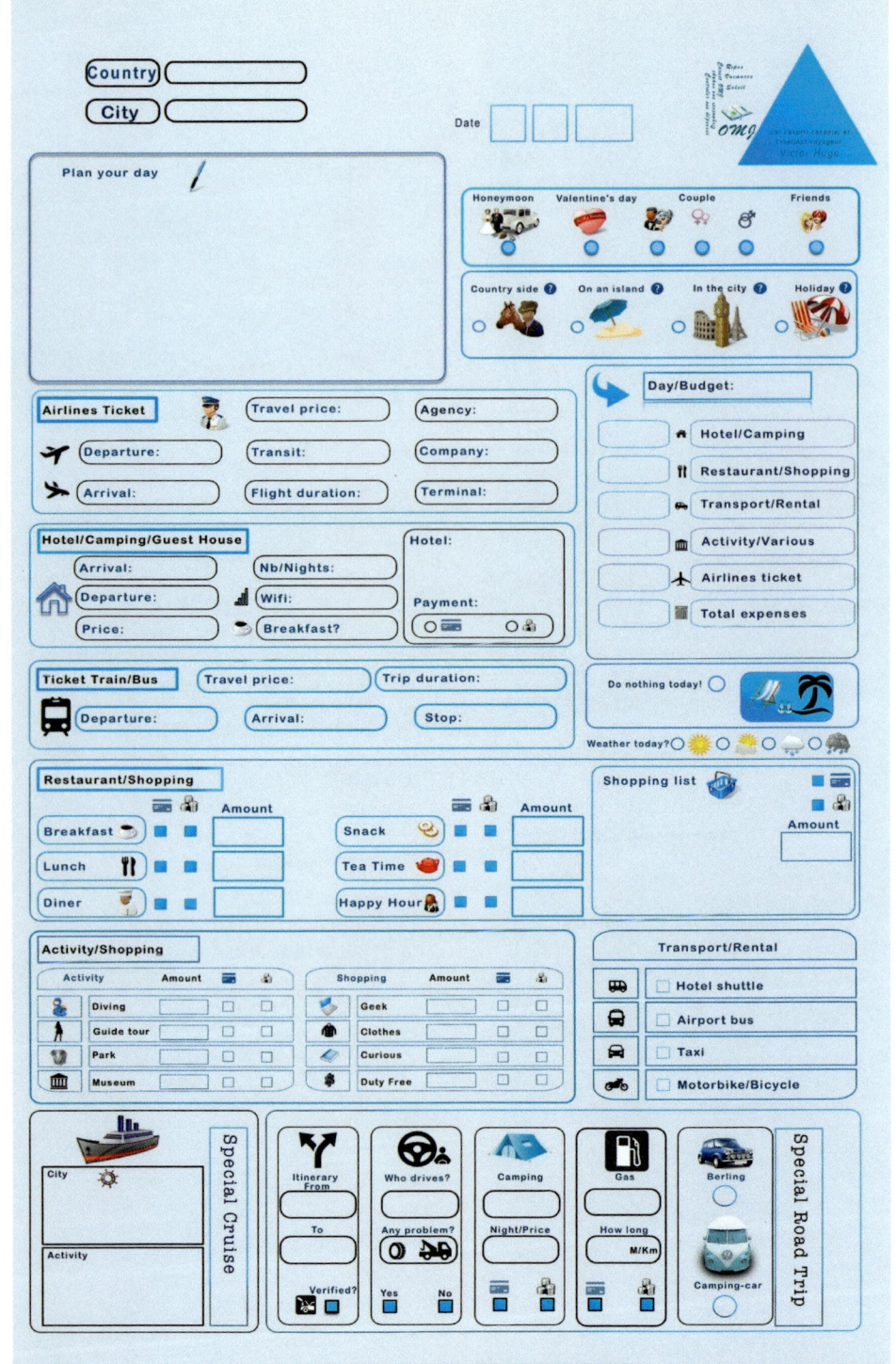

Plan your day

Honeymoon   Valentine's day   Couple   Friends

Country side   On an island   In the city   Holiday

Airlines Ticket
Travel price:
Agency:
Departure:
Transit:
Company:
Arrival:
Flight duration:
Terminal:

Hotel/Camping/Guest House
Arrival:
Nb/Nights:
Hotel:
Departure:
Wifi:
Payment:
Price:
Breakfast?

Ticket Train/Bus
Travel price:
Trip duration:
Departure:
Arrival:
Stop:

Day/Budget:
Hotel/Camping
Restaurant/Shopping
Transport/Rental
Activity/Various
Airlines ticket
Total expenses

Do nothing today!

Weather today?

Restaurant/Shopping
	Amount		Amount
Breakfast		Snack	
Lunch		Tea Time	
Diner		Happy Hour	

Shopping list
Amount

Activity/Shopping
Activity	Amount		Shopping	Amount	
Diving			Geek		
Guide tour			Clothes		
Park			Curious		
Museum			Duty Free		

Transport/Rental
Hotel shuttle
Airport bus
Taxi
Motorbike/Bicycle

Special Cruise
City
Activity

Itinerary From
To
Verified?

Who drives?
Any problem?
Yes   No

Camping
Night/Price

Gas
How long M/Km

Berling
Camping-car

Special Road Trip

How to prepare a trip.
www.vahine-production.com

Note

Bali
Chili
Mexique
Philippines
Île de Pâques
Perou
Bresil
Argentine
USA
Nouvelle-Zelande
Angleterre
Californie
Polynésie Française
Portugal
France
Corée
Cambodge
Singapour
Malaisie
Nepal
Laos
Tibet
Espagne
La Reunion
Hawaii
Les Antilles
Norvège

Thailande
Grèce Chine
Inde
Seychelles
Madagascar
Belgique
Islande
Vietnam
Italie
Australie
Japon
Danemark
Allemagne Guyane
Roumanie Taiwan
Russie
Estonie
Suisse

French Touch

Country
City
Date

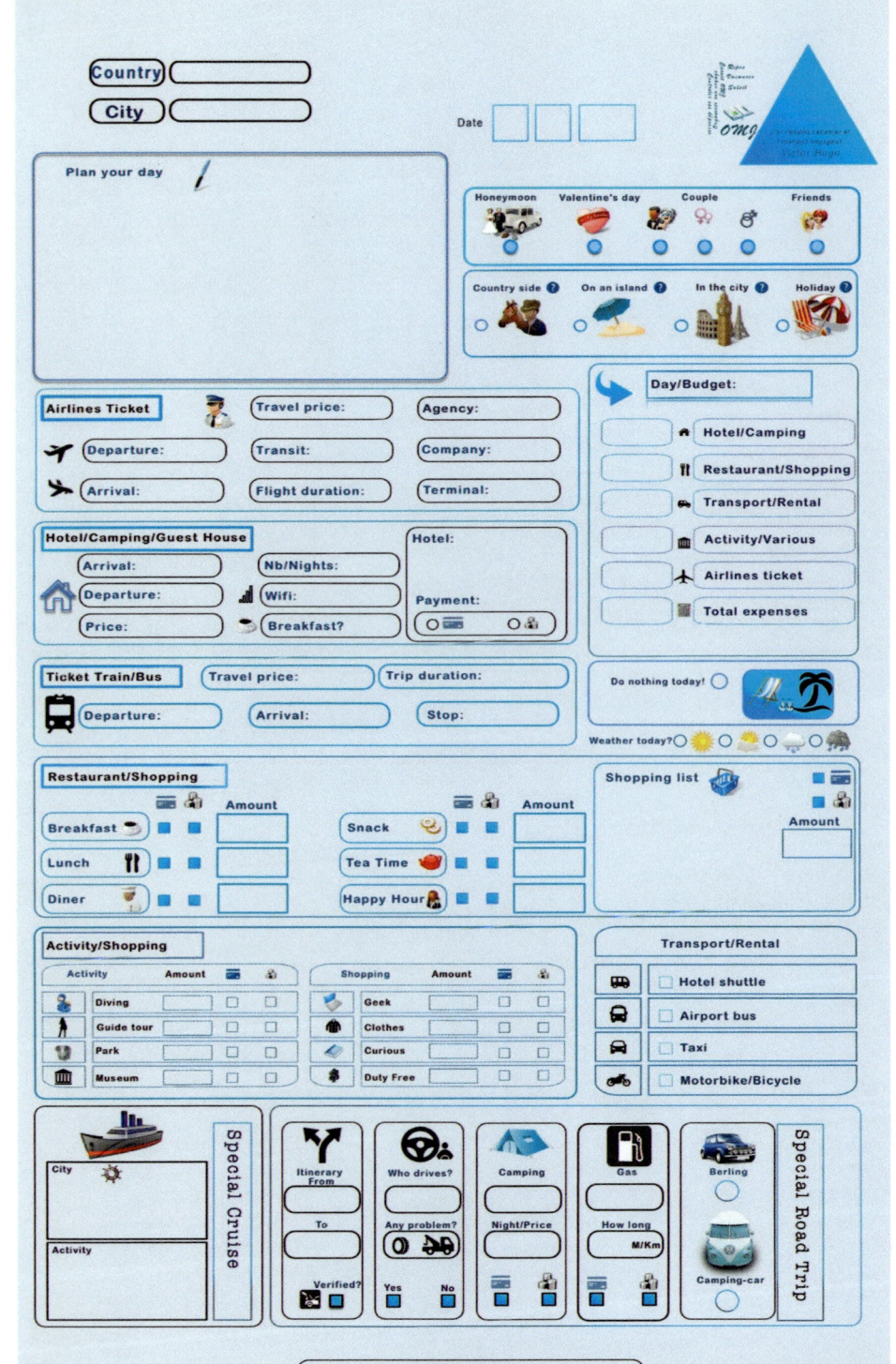

Plan your day

Honeymoon | Valentine's day | Couple | Friends

Country side | On an island | In the city | Holiday

Airlines Ticket
- Departure:
- Arrival:
- Travel price:
- Transit:
- Flight duration:
- Agency:
- Company:
- Terminal:

Hotel/Camping/Guest House
- Arrival:
- Departure:
- Price:
- Nb/Nights:
- Wifi:
- Breakfast?
- Hotel:
- Payment:

Ticket Train/Bus
- Departure:
- Travel price:
- Arrival:
- Trip duration:
- Stop:

Day/Budget:
- Hotel/Camping
- Restaurant/Shopping
- Transport/Rental
- Activity/Various
- Airlines ticket
- Total expenses

Do nothing today!

Weather today?

Restaurant/Shopping
	Amount
Breakfast	
Lunch	
Diner	
Snack	
Tea Time	
Happy Hour	

Shopping list
Amount

Activity/Shopping

Activity | Amount
- Diving
- Guide tour
- Park
- Museum

Shopping | Amount
- Geek
- Clothes
- Curious
- Duty Free

Transport/Rental
- Hotel shuttle
- Airport bus
- Taxi
- Motorbike/Bicycle

Special Cruise
- City
- Activity

- Itinerary From
- To
- Verified?

- Who drives?
- Any problem?
- Yes / No

- Camping
- Night/Price

- Gas
- How long M/Km

- Berling
- Camping-car

Special Road Trip

How to prepare a trip.
www.vahine-production.com

Note

Bali
Chili
Mexique
Îles Philippines
Pérou
Brésil
Argentine
USA
Nouvelle-Zélande
Angleterre
Californie
Polynésie Française
Portugal
Singapour
France
Corée
Cambodge
Malaisie
Nepal
Laos
Tibet
Espagne
La Réunion
Hawaii
Les Antilles
Norvège
Thailande
Grèce
Chine
Inde
Seychelles
Madagascar
Belgique
Islande
Vietnam
Italie
Australie
Japon
Danemark
Allemagne
Roumanie
Guyane
Taiwan
Russie
Estonie
Suisse

French Touch

Country

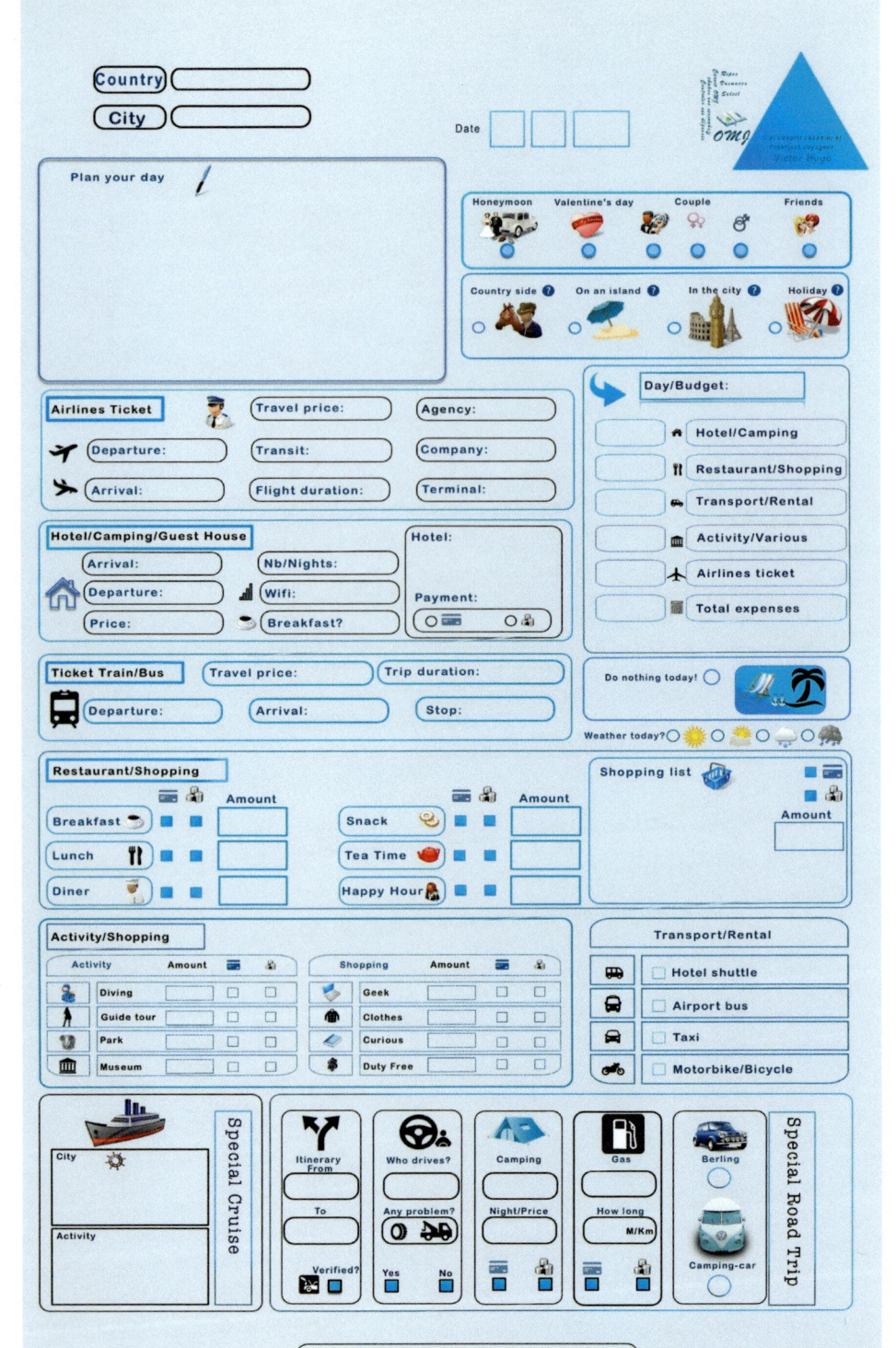

City

Date

Plan your day

Honeymoon Valentine's day Couple Friends

Country side On an island In the city Holiday

Airlines Ticket
- Travel price:
- Agency:
- Departure:
- Transit:
- Company:
- Arrival:
- Flight duration:
- Terminal:

Day/Budget:
- Hotel/Camping
- Restaurant/Shopping
- Transport/Rental
- Activity/Various
- Airlines ticket
- Total expenses

Hotel/Camping/Guest House
- Arrival:
- Nb/Nights:
- Hotel:
- Departure:
- Wifi:
- Payment:
- Price:
- Breakfast?

Ticket Train/Bus
- Travel price:
- Trip duration:
- Departure:
- Arrival:
- Stop:

Do nothing today!

Weather today?

Restaurant/Shopping
- Breakfast — Amount
- Lunch
- Diner
- Snack
- Tea Time
- Happy Hour

Shopping list — Amount

Activity/Shopping

Activity	Amount		
Diving			
Guide tour			
Park			
Museum			

Shopping	Amount		
Geek			
Clothes			
Curious			
Duty Free			

Transport/Rental
- Hotel shuttle
- Airport bus
- Taxi
- Motorbike/Bicycle

Special Cruise
- City
- Activity

- Itinerary From
- To
- Verified?

- Who drives?
- Any problem?
- Yes / No

- Camping
- Night/Price

- Gas
- How long M/Km

- Berling
- Camping-car

Special Road Trip

How to prepare a trip.
www.vahine-production.com

Note

Bali
Chili
Mexique
Philippines
Pérou
Île de Pâques
Brésil
Argentine
USA
Nouvelle-Zélande
Angleterre
Californie
Polynésie Française
Portugal
France
Singapour
Corée
Cambodge
Malaisie
Népal
Laos
Tibet
Espagne
La Réunion
Hawaii
Les Antilles
Norvège
Thaïlande
Grèce
Chine
Inde
Seychelles
Madagascar
Belgique
Islande
Vietnam
Italie
Australie
Japon
Danemark
Allemagne
Guyane
Roumanie
Taïwan
Russie
Estonie
Suisse

French Touch

Country

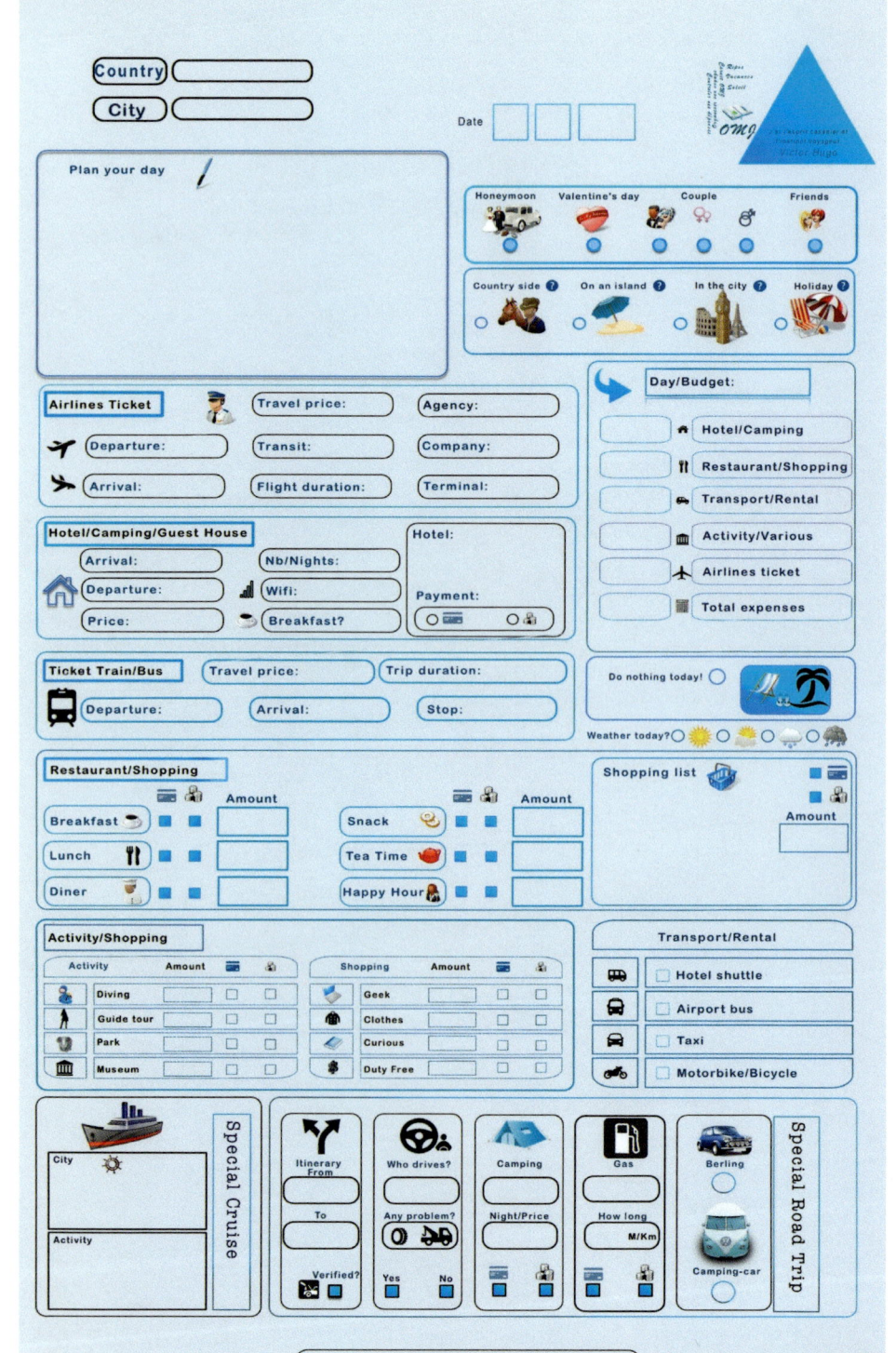

City

Date

Plan your day

Honeymoon | Valentine's day | Couple | Friends

Country side | On an island | In the city | Holiday

Day/Budget:
- Hotel/Camping
- Restaurant/Shopping
- Transport/Rental
- Activity/Various
- Airlines ticket
- Total expenses

Airlines Ticket
- Travel price:
- Agency:
- Departure:
- Transit:
- Company:
- Arrival:
- Flight duration:
- Terminal:

Hotel/Camping/Guest House
- Arrival:
- Nb/Nights:
- Hotel:
- Departure:
- Wifi:
- Payment:
- Price:
- Breakfast?

Ticket Train/Bus
- Travel price:
- Trip duration:
- Departure:
- Arrival:
- Stop:

Do nothing today!

Weather today?

Restaurant/Shopping
- Breakfast | Amount
- Lunch
- Diner
- Snack
- Tea Time
- Happy Hour

Shopping list | Amount

Activity/Shopping

Activity | Amount
- Diving
- Guide tour
- Park
- Museum

Shopping | Amount
- Geek
- Clothes
- Curious
- Duty Free

Transport/Rental
- Hotel shuttle
- Airport bus
- Taxi
- Motorbike/Bicycle

Special Cruise
- City
- Activity

- Itinerary From
- To
- Verified?

- Who drives?
- Any problem?
- Yes / No

- Camping
- Night/Price

- Gas
- How long M/Km

- Berling
- Camping-car

Special Road Trip

How to prepare a trip.
www.vahine-production.com

Note

Bali
Chili
Philippines
Île de Pâques
Mexique
Pérou
Brésil
Argentine
USA
Nouvelle-Zélande
Angleterre
Californie
Polynésie Française
Portugal
Singapour
France
Corée
Cambodge
$ Malaisie Nepal
£ Laos
¥ Tibet
€
Espagne
La Reunion
Hawaii
Les Antilles
Norvège

Thailande
Grèce Chine
Inde
Seychelles
Madagascar
Belgique
Islande
Vietnam
Italie
Australie
Japon
Danemark
Allemagne Guyane
Roumanie Russie Taiwan
Estonie
Suisse

French Touch

Country

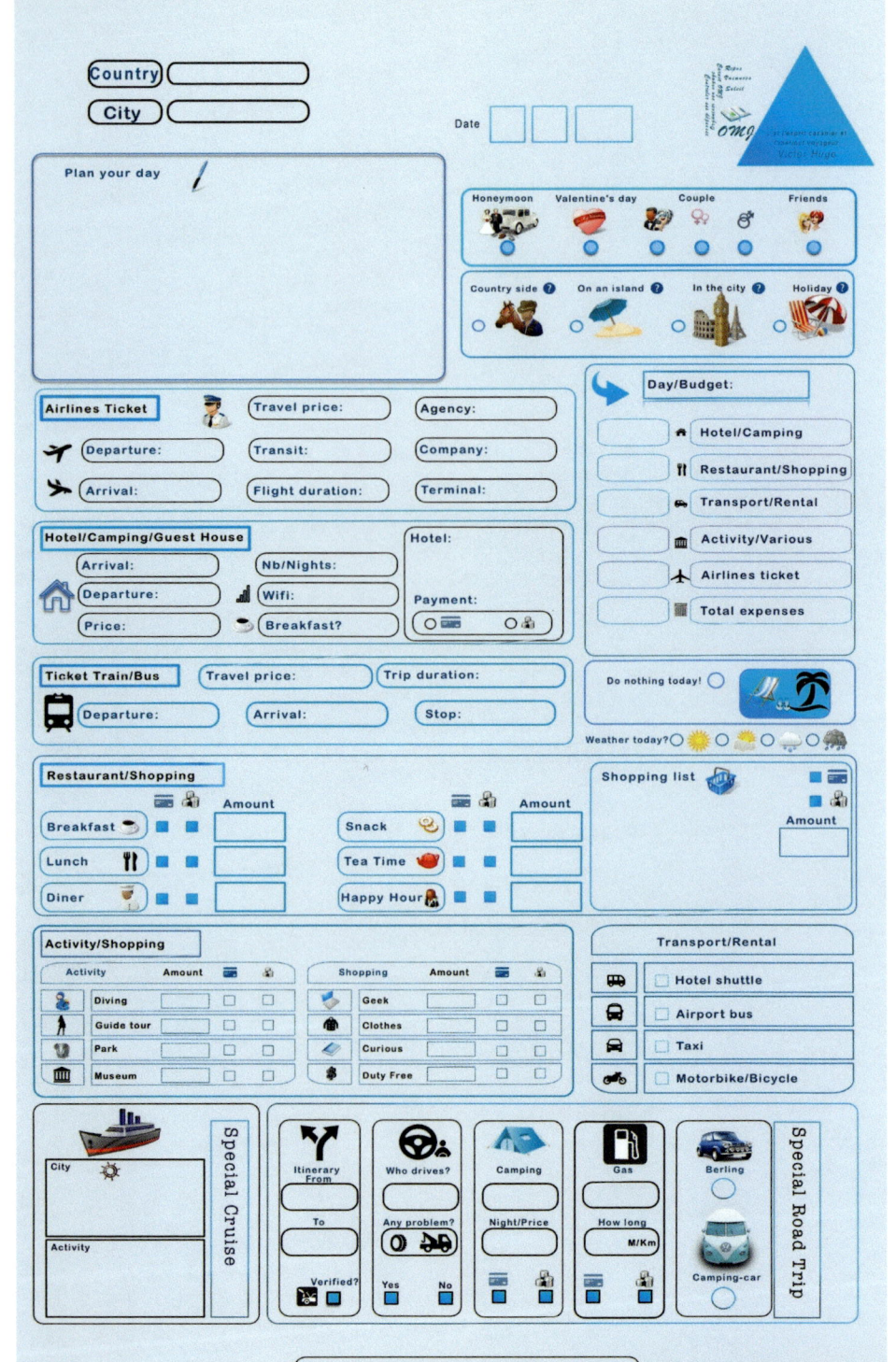

City

Date

Plan your day

Honeymoon Valentine's day Couple Friends

Country side On an island In the city Holiday

Airlines Ticket
- Travel price:
- Agency:
- Departure:
- Transit:
- Company:
- Arrival:
- Flight duration:
- Terminal:

Day/Budget:
- Hotel/Camping
- Restaurant/Shopping
- Transport/Rental
- Activity/Various
- Airlines ticket
- Total expenses

Hotel/Camping/Guest House
- Arrival:
- Nb/Nights:
- Hotel:
- Departure:
- Wifi:
- Payment:
- Price:
- Breakfast?

Ticket Train/Bus
- Travel price:
- Trip duration:
- Departure:
- Arrival:
- Stop:

Do nothing today!

Weather today?

Restaurant/Shopping
	Amount		Amount
Breakfast		Snack	
Lunch		Tea Time	
Diner		Happy Hour	

Shopping list
Amount

Activity/Shopping

Activity	Amount		Shopping	Amount	
Diving			Geek		
Guide tour			Clothes		
Park			Curious		
Museum			Duty Free		

Transport/Rental
- Hotel shuttle
- Airport bus
- Taxi
- Motorbike/Bicycle

Special Cruise
- City
- Activity

- Itinerary From
- To
- Verified?
- Who drives?
- Any problem?
- Yes / No
- Camping
- Night/Price
- Gas
- How long M/Km
- Berling
- Camping-car

Special Road Trip

How to prepare a trip.
www.vahine-production.com

Note

Bali
Chili
Mexique
Pérou
Brésil
Argentine
USA
Nouvelle-Zélande
Angleterre
Californie
Polynésie Française
Portugal
France
Corée
Cambodge
Népal
Laos
Tibet
Espagne
La Réunion
Hawaii
Les Antilles
Norvège
Thaïlande
Grèce   Chine
Inde
Seychelles
Madagascar
Belgique
Islande
Vietnam
Italie
Australie
Japon
Danemark
Guyane
Taïwan
Russie
Estonie
Suisse

Île de Pâques   Philippines
Singapour   Malaisie
Allemagne   Roumanie

French Touch

Country

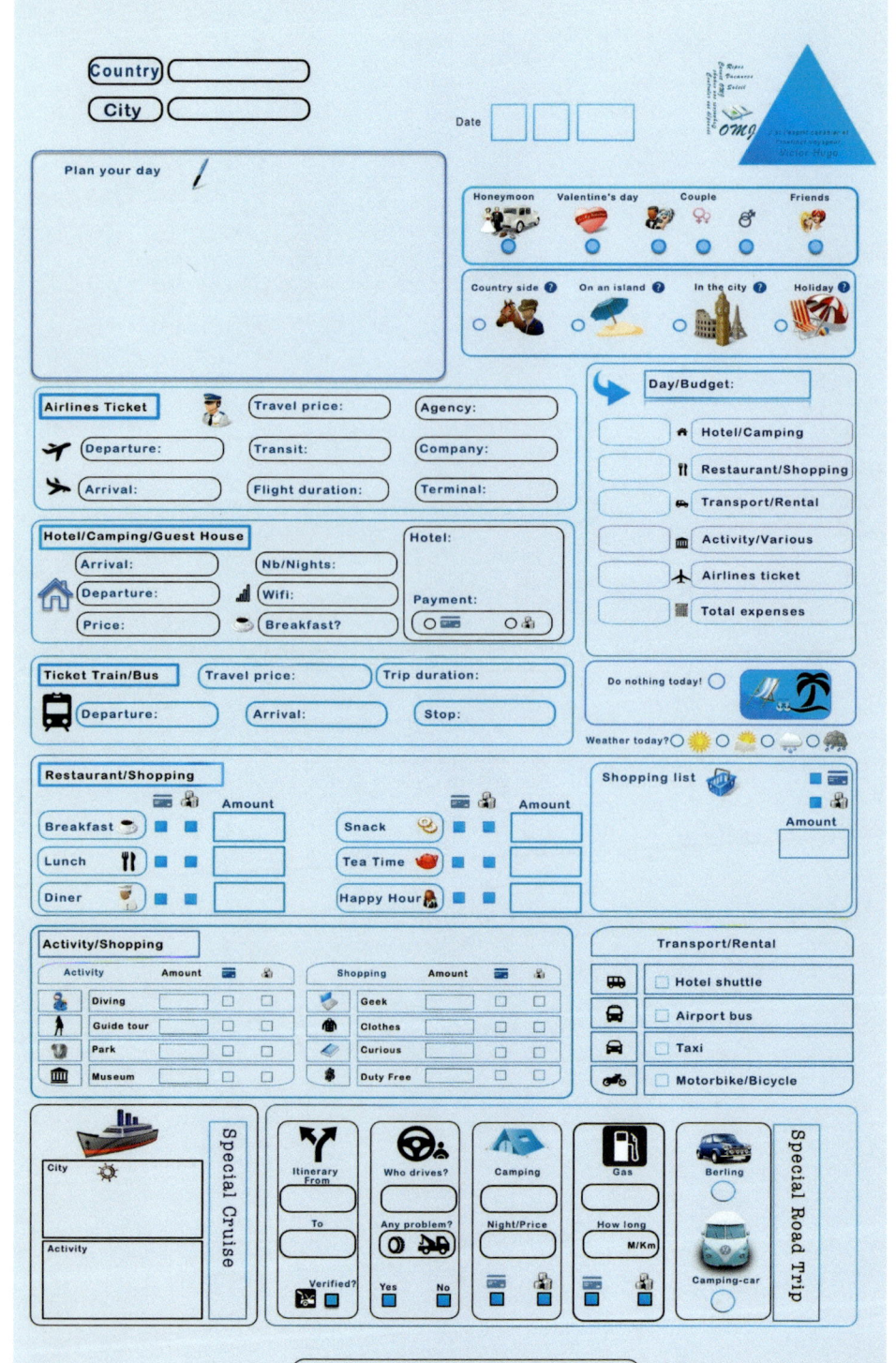

City

Date

Plan your day

Honeymoon   Valentine's day   Couple   Friends

Country side   On an island   In the city   Holiday

Airlines Ticket
Travel price: Agency:
Departure: Transit: Company:
Arrival: Flight duration: Terminal:

Hotel/Camping/Guest House
Arrival: Nb/Nights: Hotel:
Departure: Wifi: Payment:
Price: Breakfast?

Ticket Train/Bus
Travel price: Trip duration:
Departure: Arrival: Stop:

Day/Budget:
Hotel/Camping
Restaurant/Shopping
Transport/Rental
Activity/Various
Airlines ticket
Total expenses

Do nothing today!

Weather today?

Restaurant/Shopping
	Amount		Amount
Breakfast		Snack	
Lunch		Tea Time	
Diner		Happy Hour	

Shopping list
Amount

Activity/Shopping
Activity	Amount		Shopping	Amount	
Diving			Geek		
Guide tour			Clothes		
Park			Curious		
Museum			Duty Free		

Transport/Rental
Hotel shuttle
Airport bus
Taxi
Motorbike/Bicycle

City
Activity

Special Cruise

Itinerary From
To
Verified?   Yes   No

Who drives?
Any problem?

Camping
Night/Price

Gas
How long M/Km

Berling
Camping-car

Special Road Trip

How to prepare a trip.
www.vahine-production.com

Note

Bali
Chili
Philippines
Île de Pâques
Mexique
Pérou
Bresil
Argentine
USA
Nouvelle-Zelande
Angleterre
Californie
Polynésie Française
Portugal
Singapour
Malaisie
France
Corée
Cambodge
Nepal
Laos
Tibet
Espagne
La Reunion
Hawaii
Les Antilles
Norvège
Thailande
Grèce
Chine
Inde
Seychelles
Madagascar
Belgique
Islande
Vietnam
Italie
Australie
Japon
Danemark
Allemagne
Roumanie
Guyane
Taiwan
Russie
Estonie
Suisse

French Touch

Country

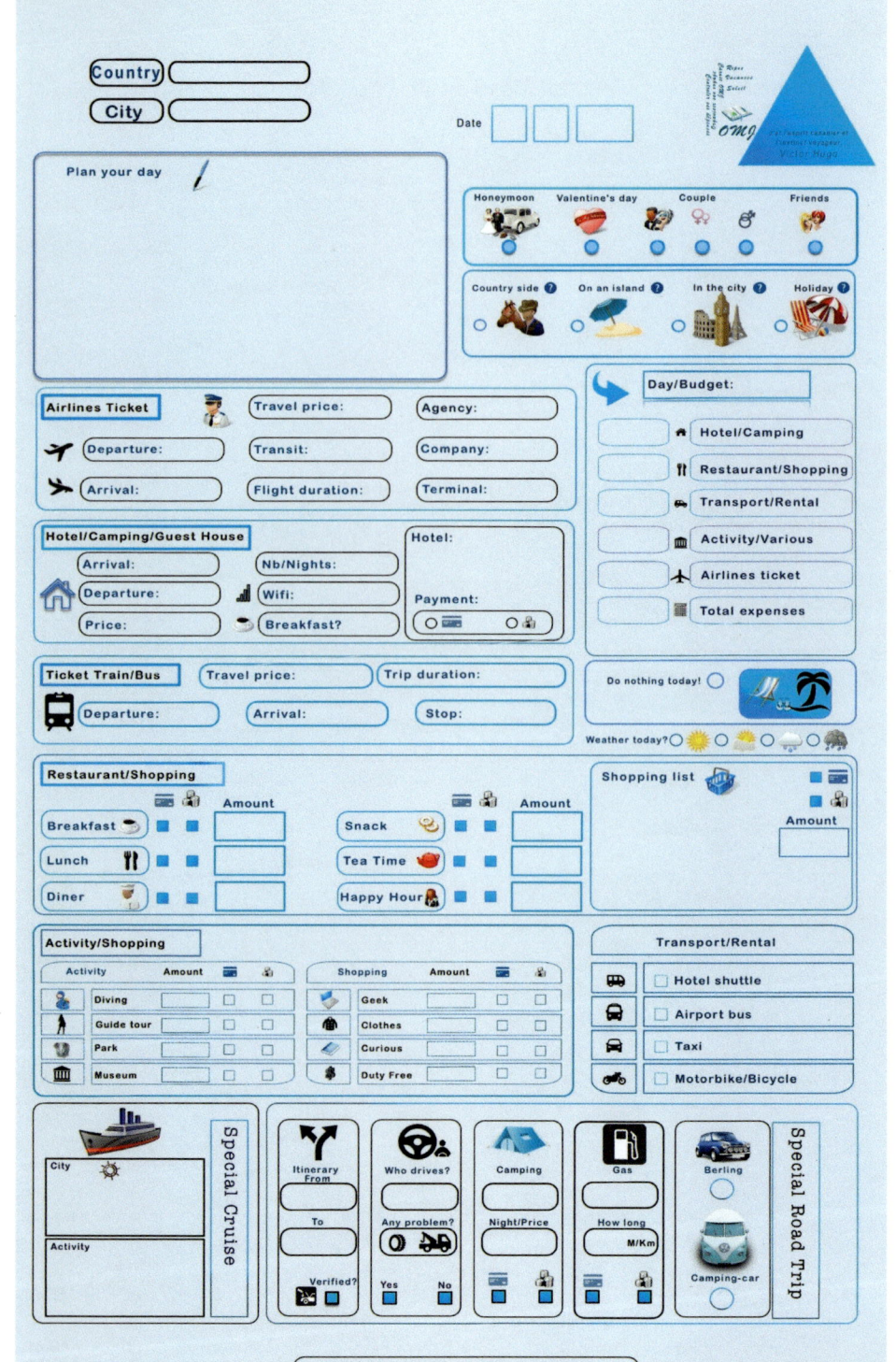

City

Date

Plan your day

Honeymoon Valentine's day Couple Friends

Country side On an island In the city Holiday

Airlines Ticket
- Departure:
- Arrival:
- Travel price:
- Transit:
- Flight duration:
- Agency:
- Company:
- Terminal:

Hotel/Camping/Guest House
- Arrival:
- Departure:
- Price:
- Nb/Nights:
- Wifi:
- Breakfast?
- Hotel:
- Payment:

Ticket Train/Bus
- Departure:
- Arrival:
- Travel price:
- Trip duration:
- Stop:

Day/Budget:
- Hotel/Camping
- Restaurant/Shopping
- Transport/Rental
- Activity/Various
- Airlines ticket
- Total expenses

Do nothing today!

Weather today?

Restaurant/Shopping
	Amount			Amount
Breakfast		Snack		
Lunch		Tea Time		
Diner		Happy Hour		

Shopping list — Amount

Activity/Shopping

Activity	Amount		Shopping	Amount	
Diving			Geek		
Guide tour			Clothes		
Park			Curious		
Museum			Duty Free		

Transport/Rental
- Hotel shuttle
- Airport bus
- Taxi
- Motorbike/Bicycle

Special Cruise
- City
- Activity

- Itinerary From
- To
- Verified?

- Who drives?
- Any problem?
- Yes / No

- Camping
- Night/Price

- Gas
- How long M/Km

Special Road Trip
- Berlingo
- Camping-car

How to prepare a trip.
www.vahine-production.com

Note

Bali
Chili
Philippines
Île de Pâques
Mexique
Perou
Bresil
Argentine
USA
Nouvelle-Zelande
Angleterre
Californie
Polynésie Française
Portugal
Singapour
France
Corée
Cambodge
$
Malaisie
Nepal
£
Laos
¥
Tibet
€
Espagne
La Reunion
Hawaii
Les Antilles
Norvège
Thailande
Grèce
Chine
Inde
Seychelles
Madagascar
Belgique
Islande
Vietnam
Italie
Australie
Japon
Danemark
Allemagne
Guyane
Roumanie
Taiwan
Russie
Estonie
Suisse

French Touch

Printed in Great Britain
by Amazon.co.uk, Ltd.,
Marston Gate.